SLINGING ARROWS

WAYNE MARDLE

SLINGING ARROWS

How
(not) to be a
professional
darts
player

EBURY
PRESS

1 3 5 7 9 10 8 6 4 2

Ebury Press, an imprint of Ebury Publishing
20 Vauxhall Bridge Road
London SW1V 2SA

Ebury Press is part of the Penguin Random House group of companies
whose addresses can be found at global.penguinrandomhouse.com

Penguin
Random House
UK

First published by Ebury Press in 2021

www.penguin.co.uk

A CIP catalogue record for this book is available from the British Library

ISBN 9781529108804

Typeset in 11.75/18.3 pt SabonNext LT Regular
by Integra Software Services Pvt. Ltd, Pondicherry

Printed and bound in Great Britain by Clays Ltd, Elcograf S.p.A.

The authorised representative in the EEA is Penguin Random House Ireland,
Morrison Chambers, 32 Nassau Street, Dublin D02 YH68

MIX
Paper from
responsible sources
FSC
www.fsc.org   FSC® C018179

Penguin Random House is committed to a sustainable
future for our business, our readers and our planet.
This book is made from Forest Stewardship Council®
certified paper.

In memory of my mum.

Miss you. Love you forever.

What a crap year 2020 was.

CONTENTS

PROLOGUE

Picture it: Rhyl, the mid-2000s. Lovable darting bon viveur Wayne Mardle (me) has come to town to take part in a darts exhibition in one of the noted seaside resort's many excellent hostelries. There's excitement in the air. Ticker-tape parades, an emergency bank holiday to mark the occasion, grown men openly weeping in the street, that sort of thing. Well, maybe not quite that sort of thing, but spirits are definitely high. And Mardle, by this point, has developed something of a reputation: in darting circles he's spoken of in hushed tones as the best double 18 hitter the world has ever seen.

Saturday night rolls around and the exhibition is going well, but as the evening wears on and alcohol has been flowing for some time, there's an interruption.

'Go on then,' one of the punters suddenly shouts. He walks over to a dartboard and slaps his hand top right, pulling his fingers apart just wide enough to reveal the double 18. 'If you think you're so good, let's see a double 18 right now.'

'Let's not do this,' Mardle says.

'Come on,' the other fella roars. 'Prove how good you are.'

Mardle is, understandably, concerned about how this is panning out. 'I do miss sometimes,' our hero says. 'I don't want to hit you.'

'I'm not moving until you do it.'

Someone starts asking Mardle about personal liability insurance, but by this point two hundred people are gathered round, baying for the future world darts almost-champion to work his magic. There's no way out for Mardle, who has no option but to take his shot. He settles into his stance, draws his wrist back and releases the dart, which smashes straight through the fella's index finger.

The room falls silent, save for the distinctive, elongated howl of a man whose finger is now pinned to the dartboard. He uses his other hand to pull the dart out; he then walks over to Mardle and hands back the dart. As he does so, he offers two words – 'Thanks, Wayne!' – and a smile. The evening continues.

If you're planning a career in darts, that's the sort of bewildering situation you should be prepared to encounter with alarming frequency. In fact, accidentally popping a dart through a fan's hand is one of the more everyday occurrences of life in the darts lane.

Over the years I've seen things you wouldn't believe. I've seen Phil Taylor's face tattooed on the shoulder of a darts fan. I watched Bobby George's shirts glitter in the dark at the Circus Tavern. Those moments may be lost in time, but in *Slinging Arrows* I hope I'll bring you closer than you've ever been, and possibly slightly closer than you might ever have wanted, to the true experience of life as an international darting specialist. In the following pages you'll find:

- 🎯 Tips on how to compete against any opponent, from your local boozer to the world stage.
- 🎯 Advice on how to trash a hotel room, but politely.
- 🎯 An extended portion regarding underwear.
- 🎯 A cautionary tale regarding the impact on your performance of a forty-eight-hour Vegas bender prior to a globally televised world final.
- 🎯 The not strictly darts-related, but at the same time not entirely unreasonable claim that anyone who makes their tea 'milk first' is a psychopath.

You'll laugh. You'll cry. You'll find yourself searching YouTube for a clip of me accidentally letting rip with a string of expletives on Dutch television.

But most of all I hope you feel a sense of possibility. There's never a bad time to pick up your first dart, take part in your first tournament or join your first darts league. Darts was my first love and it remains the friendliest, warmest and most human experience I've ever encountered. It's where I've made friends for life and met the world's most extraordinary people. It's a sport, it's a hobby, it's entertainment, but most importantly to me it's a way of life, and one whose sense of camaraderie and family I simply wouldn't swap for anything.

And there's nothing to stop you getting involved right now. The darts I used for my entire professional career were a set my dad picked up for me in 1983, from a guy in the Clothworkers Arms in Islington, and they cost £3. So have a rummage down the back of your sofa and see what spare change you come up with, then join me on the oche and let's get throwing.

1.

EQUIPMENT

I'm one of those sportsmen who likes to take time out from the highs and lows of one sport by getting involved in the highs and lows of another, and before I set off to The Belfry or Loch Lomond for a round of golf there's nothing I find more enjoyable than the detailed rigmarole of getting my bag ready. I lose myself in the reverie of ritual and preparation, getting everything just right: Ray-Bans in the compartment I always put them in, a dozen new Titleist Pro V1 golf balls, suncream in the side pocket, the whole lot. I can spend hours fussing over getting ready, and when I'm done I'll look proudly at the bag, and the clubs that have been given a little run-over with a damp cloth, and I'll know the kit will do well for me that day. I'm like the proud farmer at the end of *Babe*. 'That'll do, bag full of golf paraphernalia. That'll do.'

When it comes to darts there's significantly less ceremony: I get them out of my pocket, check nothing's bent and get on with it. Too small to admire – that's the problem with darts. (Not something you can necessarily say about some of the guys who throw them, but I'll deal with fitness in another chapter.)

The point is that compared with a lot of sports people I can travel extraordinarily lightly. And much like a double thumbs-up from the titular character of an eighties TV show about a retired fireman turned motorcycling private investigator, that's a positive boon. Whether I'm performing in a tournament or at a darts exhibition I can simply arrive at the venue, the arena, the pub, the club or the conference centre with my Hawaiian shirt on under my jacket and darts in my pocket, and be ready to go. Sometimes people who work at venues just can't believe it.

'Do you need anywhere to get ready?' they'll ask. 'Do you want to put your stuff somewhere?'

I'm like: 'I'm ready, all the stuff I need is in my pocket, let's go.'

Afterwards it's a question of putting the darts back in the pocket, getting the jacket back on, then sauntering off out of the venue: job done. I've seen players leave a stage and within thirty seconds they've exited the building. GONE.

Travelling light is a perk of the job, and when I see the alternative I come out in a cold sweat. I was at Atlanta airport fifteen years ago and saw a team of shooters turn up with boxes literally full of guns – as you'd expect, they were given an armed escort around the entire place. I said to one of them: 'You've really got your work cut out for you here.' I mean, that's not going to be an easy chat at check-in, is it?

'Did you pack this bag yourself, sir?'

'Yes, I did.'

'Does it contain any dangerous weapons?'

'Yes, as a matter of fact it does, it's basically a load of guns.'

I feel quite bad for professional anglers too, with the lengthy equipment they need to sling over their shoulder and transport from place to place, although I suppose you could say they've made a rod for their own back.

When I say I travel light I mean precisely 66 grams light – that's the weight of three 22-gram darts. The weight of a dart can vary wildly, from about 10g (also roughly the amount of fat you might expect to find in a standard, non-multipack chocolate bar) all the way up to 48g. There's no right or wrong weight for a dart and you'll find the full spectrum when it comes to professional players: Stephen 'The Bullet' Bunting, a former world champion, uses 12g, whereas Ryan Searle got the nickname Heavy Metal for a reason – he prefers a 32g dart. There's no beef between players who go for different weights; as a professional dartist you wouldn't think less of someone who uses a really heavy dart or a really light one. I mean, you might wonder how the hell someone throws their ridiculous implement, but different weights work for different players, and that's that.

The size of a dart is of particular concern when you're trying to get three of them into a very small space – which, if you're going for a treble 20, is always. Darts have actually changed in size over the years due to developments in how they're made and what they're made of. The brass darts that were popular until the 1970s were, quite frankly, enormous.

Back then a 22g brass dart would be about 10mm wide, but after manufacturing moved to darts that are predominantly tungsten – which has the benefit of being cheap and easy to manufacture – a 22g dart ended up being half the size.

You'll find copper and nickel in those darts too, but the general rule is that the higher the percentage of tungsten, the smaller your dart's likely to be. When you bear in mind that the width of a wire on the dartboard – less than a millimetre – is the difference between champ and chump, you can understand how the smaller darts we're seeing now are resulting in statistics like we've never seen before.

Some people might argue that making it easier to hit a treble 20 today is, in some way, unfair to the players of yesteryear in that it's resulted in a kind of inflation in how well players can do – a bit like making a goal twice as big in football, then being surprised when all the subsequent matches suddenly end up with scores like 20–13. Then again, I think about those footballs like sacks of sand that we used to get whacked at us at school in the seventies, when I'd refuse every header and simply get out of the way if someone passed to me, and then I think of the featherweight balls the professionals play with in 2021, and I feel like that's more of an appropriate comparison. And whatever equipment you happen to be using, consistently hitting treble 20s and doubles is the same as scoring a hat-trick in a World Cup final: maybe easier than it was fifty years ago, but still not *that* easy, and impossible to most.

When you've found your ideal dart weight, the next thing to consider is the grip of the dart. You'll find grips billed as 'knurled', 'concave', 'aggressive' and so on. Some of these fancy designs are just absolute nonsense, serving no practical purpose whatsoever, and are there purely for aesthetics. One thing you'll find most professionals have in common is that they all stick to the basics of everything. Watch the World Championship and you'll see the players' stems are quite mundane and there are hardly any funky grips going on.

Extravagant-looking darts are more for the consumer rather than the pro, but for consumers there's never been so much choice. It's got to the point where they're selling exactly the same dart in different colours, in the hope that they might sell more if some happen to be purple and some happen to be a slightly different shade of purple. And you might say to me: 'Wayne, isn't that exactly what you're doing with your own range of darts?' And in my defence I'd say this: as ridiculous as it might look when you see a load of otherwise identical darts lined up in a shop, I actually like the different colours. Just because the pros stick to the boring basics, that doesn't mean fans can't have a bit of fun. If a customer loves the look of it, what's the problem?

Truth is, we all buy things with our eyes first. And psychologically if you're happy with what you've got, you'll gain confidence, and it'll give you a better game ... Or at least you'll think it will, and that in itself can be an advantage. The long and short of it is this: whether it's a car, a dart or a kettle, if you put a load of men in a room with something that can in some small way be customised for no logical reason, they'll throw everything and the kitchen sink at making it as complicated as possible.

'Do we need a third window wiper on this new car design?'

'No.'

'Will it sell?'

'Yes.'

'Let's do it.'

That's all fine by me. One thing I have noticed, though, is that while players now have a lot of different darts to choose from, the cost varies hugely too. If you're looking into buying a new set of darts you'll find yourself dazzled by the range of prices. You can spend a fiver on a set, or a hundred times that. Long gone are the days when darts were made on a lathe in a shed by some bloke called Bert. I wonder what's happened to Bert now? I expect he probably retired. Maybe he's long gone.

How much you want to spend on your darts is totally up to you. Target's Elysian darts go for half a grand – they're truly beautiful and absolutely fantastic feats of engineering which people often treat as collector's items rather than things you'd throw in the pub, but you don't need to take out a second mortgage to get a dart that's going to do the job. There's a point somewhere between the £5 set and the £500 after which the extra money's not really adding much.

Think about it like this – you'd feel the difference between a fifteen-grand car and one that costs a hundred grand. As for the ones in between, there's a point somewhere past the fifty-grand mark where you're not likely to be really noticing much difference. In darts, that point's far closer to the £5 set than the £500 set! In golf I've used cheap clubs as well as clubs worth a thousand quid – it's nice to hold the pricier ones, and it's clear you're holding quality, but I've noticed precisely no difference in the actual game I play, which is to say I'm mediocre either way.

You'll likely find something similar with your darts. The fact that my dad paid three quid for the darts that lasted me my entire career should tell you everything you need to know. It didn't matter how much they'd cost. The point was that those darts – 80 per cent tungsten, 20 per cent nickel – felt smooth enough for me to throw, with enough grip for me to be able to propel. They felt like an extension of my fingers, and that's how you want your own dart to feel.

All you really want is to know your dart's going to fly from A to B (A being your hand, B being the dartboard). (If you're having trouble remembering which is A and which is B, remember 'hand' has the letter A in it, and 'dartboard' has the letter B in it, and while dartboard also has the letter A in it, that A appears twice and therefore cancels itself out.) (You're welcome.)

When it comes to looking after your point there's a myth that every single player on the planet should do one thing when they get their darts out of the case: sharpen them. 'Points need to be sharp', they say. This, I'm afraid, is absolute nonsense, but what points *do* need is to be rough enough to stay in the board.

The player Roland Scholten was always notable for many reasons – the background of his nickname Tripod is too graphic to go into here, he used to come out to 'Are You Gonna Go My Way' by Lenny Kravitz, and at six foot seven he loomed over the rest of us – but my abiding memory of Scholten is that the first time I ever clapped eyes on him in a practice room somewhere in the world, he was sitting in a chair, bolt upright, legs crossed, roughening up his points. He used to do it meticulously. It was almost like some sort of yogic meditation ritual. I haven't seen him play for the best part of ten years and that's still the image I have of him.

You don't need to go The Full Scholten, but every darts player should rub a little bit of emery cloth up and down the point for four seconds. Actually, we're all busy people, so let's call it two seconds. Up and down, job done. A simple operation, but it'll save you 60 points here and there. Even some pros don't know this, but now I'm retired I can put it in print without it impacting my ranking.

While some aspects of the dart, like the barrel, won't directly affect your action, the flight is a different matter. All in there are about twenty different shapes, each in various thicknesses and it's a case of trial and error before you arrive on the one that's right for you. Back in the day flights were made of feathers or cardboard. Mind you, so was nearly everything until the 1960s. The point is that it was extremely rare to have two flights exactly the same. These days flights are cut by machines rather than by hand, with huge units churning out thousands per hour. This has been helpful for the game: darts players all want consistency, and you simply can't be consistent with inconsistent material. I'd go so far as to say that the flight is the most important part of the whole set-up because the right (or wrong) flight will affect not just how the dart flies through the air but also – the important bit – where it ends up.

It's important that your dart enters the board at an angle you like. Once you've settled on that angle, you need to find a flight that helps you achieve it. I like my darts to point up to the ceiling a little, and a standard flight gives me what I'm after. Generally speaking the bigger the flight, the slower the dart goes through the air. There's more contact with the air, isn't there? Or something? Look, I'm not an aeronautics specialist and the closest I've come to being an expert in drag and thrust relates to a wig and a misunderstanding on a stag do in the late nineties, but it's safe to say that if you were to stick a seven-foot flight in a dart, it wouldn't go very fast.

While I'm generally prepared to live and let live with equipment, I do have a nomination for worst flight ever. It's one that's entirely useless to a normal human being. You might as well not be using a flight at all: it's so small that it gives you no stability whatsoever, it causes the dart to spiral out of control and it offers, in my opinion, more problems than anything else. And that's the 9Five G5. The flight Phil Taylor uses – and he's the most successful player in history. Go, as they say in the good ol' Uncle US of Stateside, figure. I do sometimes wonder how much better Phil might have been if he'd used a decent flight – it doesn't bear thinking about, to be honest, and it was probably best for the rest of us that he stuck with the G5s. But joking aside, you do need to be truly gifted to throw using those things.

At this juncture I feel it's also worth apologising to anybody in the darts community who may have seen a promotion I was involved with a few years back in which I appeared to endorse a less than supreme set of flights. Well, I say I 'appeared' to endorse them – I literally did say they were great. I was sponsored by Target Darts at the time and after they sent me flights for review I went back to them letting them know that in my review I'd be stating that the flights in question should not necessarily be used by a player hoping for success. Target helpfully pointed out that they were paying me to help them increase sales and suggested politely, but really rather firmly, that I reconsider my review. So if you bought the flights based on the *second* version of my review, I do apologise – I was being paid, and I'm a mercenary.

If you're going to be practising at home you'll also be wanting to get your own dartboard. Back in the day there used to be a type of board called the elm board – basically, and there's a clue in the name, it was a slice of elm tree trunk with a dartboard printed on it. That's the sort of thing you might have found in a boozer fifty years ago, but it wasn't exactly low maintenance and to keep its integrity they used to have to soak it in a bucket of water overnight, then dry it out for a day so they could then play on it a day later. That might have been workable in the 1950s, when there was nothing to do with your time other than sit around a fire playing the lute, but in the twenty-first century we've got busy lives and moistening a tree trunk to make it usable isn't top of anyone's list when it comes to recreation.

These days, boards are more commonly made of paper and cork, but the majority of boards you'll see everywhere from pubs to the telly are made from a plant called sisal. There's some degree of manufacture involved, of course – people aren't employed to pluck ready-formed dartboards off trees. I appreciate the Venn diagram of darts enthusiasts and botany fans doesn't involve a huge amount of crossover, so here are the main things you need to know about sisal:

1. Its proper name is *Agave Sisalana*, which coincidentally is also the name of the bloke who came third in the 2004 Eurovision Song Contest.

2. Sisal is used in making rope, carpets and bags, in other words everything you need to effectively dispose of a body.

3. Off the top of my head and having made absolutely no visits to Wikipedia to research this, I can also tell you that in East Africa, where production is typically on large estates,[citation needed] the leaves are transported to a central decortication plant, where water is used to wash away the waste parts of the leaf.[10]

To be honest I feel all the dartboard manufacturers are missing a bit of a trick here. You can't move these days for people advertising their products as being organic, and the first dartboard manufacturer to go the whole hog on this will clean up. A selling point's a selling point, right?

The thing with sisal is that no matter how well a board's constructed, it's never totally predictable. Because it's made out of a plant the dartboard can move, shift, grow, shrink and change overnight. It might be stored somewhere damp, so it'll expand; in a dry place it can wilt. I hope this doesn't offend any sisal crusaders but it's not the most consistent plant, and because of this you can get an unexpected dead spot on a dartboard: you're playing a match, you've got the full glare of the world's media and some commentator like me whipping viewers into a frenzy over this pivotal throw, the dart goes in ... and then it falls straight out again. So as the dart flops to the floor, the player who looked, three seconds ago, like he or she could go on to be a world champion, suddenly doesn't look so hot any more.

If you follow darts on social media you'll have seen fans having a right old go at one brand in particular for this. Unicorn were the best manufacturers of darts and dartboards for decades; these days they have way more competition, but their dartboards are still very good, to such an extent that they're the only dartboards we see on TV. And because they're the only ones we see on TV, if there's a malfunctioning one, and for instance a dart happens to fall out of the bullseye, Unicorn get stick on social media. You'll get the managing director of another company subtweeting them and all sorts. It's absolutely pathetic, to be honest, but Unicorn always bite their tongues when it's kicking off – they've been in the industry too long to get involved in those shenanigans. They're a classy outfit.

Anyway, it's worth remembering that when a dart falls out, nine times out of ten you can't blame the player. It's happened to the best of us – a perfectly thrown dart rejected on the whim of some fibrous south Mexican vegetation. I do feel that there's something poetic happening here. That perhaps there's something about this scenario bigger than the simple matter of some fella on the oche chucking a dart at a wall. Bigger than any of us.

It's the engineered steel of the dart, versus the soft sisal of the board. It's industry versus nature, with man caught in between. I'm generally more Tuborg than Thunberg, but could we see the sisal's occasional rejection of the dart as a metaphor for nature fighting back against what mankind has done to our beautiful planet? Is the rebellious dartboard, pushing back on the relentless march of progress, any different to the wild bear who attacks the disrespectful tourist? The fierce, roaring waves of the sea that punish and pummel the legs of a polluting oil rig?

Obviously it doesn't matter *what* your board's made of if it's not in the right place. The PDC (Professional Darts Corporation – more on them later) are very clear on the rules here: the board must be hung so that the bullseye is five feet and eight inches from the floor, with the oche seven feet and 9.25 inches away. It's incredibly precise.

Generally in life I'd say a quarter of an inch here or there doesn't make too much difference (ooh missus, etc.) in relation to the player's distance *from* the board, but when it comes to the height there really must be consistency. And that's not something you can ever take for granted. Russ Bray, the noted darts referee, and I were once hired to perform at a wedding reception in Holland – we'd been booked as entertainment in much the same way one might book a covers band or local DJ, which felt strange but the newlyweds both loved darts and they wanted me at their wedding, and more importantly they were paying and there was free food, so off we went. It was a lovely wedding but the board was so high that the treble 20 was about nine feet off the ground, making it at least three feet too high. I actually had to jump up to get my darts out. I finished, miraculously, on 170 – the Big Fish – but more through luck than judgement. The whole episode was ridiculous, but I did my job: played the bride, played the groom, then tucked into the roast hog and said no more about the sky-high dartboard.

At the other extreme I once found myself employed by Ladbrokes to go round their shops and do a couple of hours here and there to entertain the punters. I turned up at one shop, which to save some blushes I'll just say was in the south-west of England, and when I got there the dartboard was propped against a coffee machine, four feet off the ground. I did the whole thing with people wandering backwards and forwards in front of me while they got a drink, and had to keep stopping to warn them not to burn themselves.

(Sidenote: the proper height of a dartboard is about the same height as a human face so if you're starting out at home please, for the love of God, think twice about hanging the board on the back of your bedroom door. I know parents can be annoying when you're a teenager and we all need our private space at that age so you could argue that learning to knock would be helpful, but your dad deserves better than a dart in the eye just for bringing in your laundry.)

One last point on positioning: the way a board's attached to the wall is pretty important too. I once did an exhibition in someone's garden for a fiftieth birthday party and they'd attached a dartboard to the side of their shed (fine) by hammering a four-inch nail through the bullseye (you what?). It was stable enough: top marks for that. That board absolutely was not going anywhere. But I'll tell you what was also not happening: a bullseye finish.

I did point this out to the bloke whose birthday it was and, quite brilliantly, he replied: 'Oh, it's fine, we never hit the bullseye.'

'Well, you might not mate,' I said, 'but I'd probably have had a chance.'

Finally, I couldn't finish this chapter without considering the thorny issue of soft-tipped darts. I say 'thorny' – a literal bit of old spiky bush would have a better chance of sticking in a real dartboard than soft-tipped darts which, and I promise I won't go on about this, I'm not that keen on.

If you're going down this route you'll need a special dartboard full of thousands of tiny holes that a plastic dart, with its plastic wobbly tip, is supposed to stick into; and because it's made out of plastic it can have all sorts of electronics in the board to keep score and so on, plus you can connect it to your phone or tablet for reasons it'd have taken hours to explain to my dad's generation of darts players. I've always had a view that soft-tipped darts (which, just to reiterate, I'm not that keen on) are for players who just want to rock up and have a bit of fun, which is fine in and of itself but, let's be serious now, it's all barely one step up from those velcro darts sets you win at the fair. A non-thinking man's darts. Childish, even. I do apologise if you feel I'm repeating myself here, but I'll just say it one more time in case you missed it earlier: I'm not that keen.

That said, while I'm never likely to totally change my view on soft-tipped darts (my view, for the avoidance of doubt, being that I'm not keen), I did come close to reconsidering a year or so back when I was asked to be one manufacturer's worldwide ambassador. They sent me a unit over: I fitted it up, played on it for a couple of hours, and do you know what? It was amazing fun. It lit up, it made noises, there were LED screens going off and stampeding buffalo running around all over the place. Everything went nuts in vivid pinks and pastel blues. I felt like I was at a rave. It was an audiovisual extravaganza.

But it was just not darts, or darts as I know it. I suppose I think of it like I think of the difference between snooker and pool – I can guarantee you snooker players will tell you pool's easier than snooker: not proper, somehow. And do you know what? It is easier, and it's *not* proper. Steel-tip darts is harder than soft-tip darts because the segments are smaller, and that's just a fact. That said, there's no denying the whole soft-tip thing is a big business. Once a year they play a world championship soft-tip event and the winner gets $100k. That's a lot of money. Proper money, regardless of how you view soft-tip darts. (My view: not keen.)

2.

NICKNAMES

If you want to be taken seriously as a darts player, or even if you want the sort of career I had, you will be needing to sort yourself out with a nickname. Nicknames find their way into most sports but it's darts in which these names really do come to define your entire life, and it's darts in which you'll find grown men calling themselves things like The Spanish Assassin, Hotdog, Mr Muscle, The Womble, and The Ferret. (I made Mr Muscle up of course – Mr Muscle is a fair-to-middling brand of oven cleaner and sink unblocker, although the fact that it fits right in with the real ones says all you need to know about darting nicknames.)

Nicknames in darts have been around since the 1970s, and it's no coincidence that this was also the period in which darts became a big thing on TV. In the intervening years some nicknames have aged better than others – Eric Bristow was one of the first with The Crafty Cockney, a true classic of the genre, but then there's my good mate and favourite person in the world Bobby George, well known on the scene for his spangly stage attire, who back in the day decided to go with the name

Mr Glitter. In recent years it's become very clear that the Glitter gang is one you most definitely do not wanna be in, so it's probably best all round that Bobby later chose to go by The King of Bling.

Choosing an appropriate *nom de fléchettes* is an art form in its own right. Many nicknames, like The Crafty Cockney, make perfect sense due to a combination of personality and geography, although it's less well known that Bristow's name actually came from the fact that he used to visit a pub called the Crafty Cockney in LA. People identified that he was crafty and a cockney, and you might argue he was both, but the Crafty Cockney was simply where he drank and played darts when Stateside.

Some nicknames are location based, some are a pun on the player's name, some rhyme, some simply look funny. An amount of alliteration's always an advantage, also. Irony's a good bet, too – Jarkko Komula is nicknamed Smiley on account of the fact that he spends most of the time with a face like a slapped derrière on a wet Wednesday.

My first nickname was Mouth of the South, which worked on a few levels: I was from the south of England, it rhymed, and I had – and still have – a fully functioning oral cavity. But after I started wearing Hawaiian shirts and chose the *Hawaii Five-O* theme as my walk-on music, Bobby George cornered me.

'So,' he said, 'you've got a Hawaiian shirt, you've got the *Hawaii Five-O* theme tune, and darts legs start with a score of 501. Why don't you call yourself Hawaii 501?'

'Don't be ridiculous,' I said.

'That's absolutely genius,' I thought.

I rarely give Bobby credit for this because I've decided he doesn't deserve it and that all the glory should fall to me. But Hawaii 501 really was genius, and still is. Even today I get a tweet here and there whenever someone's been watching *Hawaii Five-O* on TV, but in answer to your next question no, I've never been to Hawaii and I'll tell you why: it's too bloody far. It takes eleven hours to get to LA, then another six to get to Hawaii. Not a chance.

Hawaii 501 worked because it was a collision of multiple factors. In a similar ballpark was Bob Anderson, the 1988 World Champion, who used to wear cowboy shirts and called himself the Limestone Cowboy, a name bestowed upon him by legendary commentator Sid Waddell on account of Anderson's relationship with Wiltshire and its limestone hills.

Anderson really picked up that idea and ran with it, or at least trotted with it. As well as regularly walking on to Glen Campbell's 'Rhinestone Cowboy' there was the legendary moment at the 1995 PDC World Championship when Bob appeared on stage at the Circus Tavern accompanied by a horse. A full-on, actual horse. The sort of horse where you see it and go: 'That right there is a *horse*.' None of which could have been predicted by Sid Waddell when he made that first tentative suggestion that Limestone Cowboy might make a good moniker, but it just goes to show the unintended consequences of an innocuous nickname. It's the butterfly effect in action. Deep in a rainforest a darts commentator flaps his arms around; somewhere else in the world a horse appears on stage at a strip club.

Sadly for me, and you know I like to put on a show, the process of actually announcing your first nickname, or a new one, is frustratingly underwhelming. You simply tell a few people what it is, and let the darts gossip network do the rest. In an ideal world when a name choice has been made I'd like to see the darts community take a leaf out of the Catholic Church's book, acknowledging the conclusion of the decision-making process by releasing a plume of white smoke. I appreciate many darts players these days may live in apartments and new builds without chimneys, but we're living in a glorious era in which you can pick up a perfectly functional garden incinerator from B&Q for £21, so there's really no reason for anyone to feel left out.

As for the reveal itself, I feel more of a song and dance should be made of the whole affair, and by that I literally mean there should be a song and a dance. If parents-to-be can pull off pyrotechnic-filled, Broadway-scale gender-reveal parties for babies when the outcome is rarely a surprise because in the majority of cases the 'reveal' is going to be one of just two outcomes, imagine the scale of the spectacle and the feeling of excitement that could accompany a darts player's new name when the name in question could be absolutely *anything*.

And it literally could be anything. Welsh player Ritchie Davies was called Lambchop, for instance, which might have been better if he'd also been into karate, although that whole concept was already sewn up by Kirk 'Martial Dartist' Shepherd, who would often arrive on stage with some sort of karate kick.

Elsewhere I'm rather fond of the name I gave to Ricky 'Rapid' Evans, a man who is, without a doubt, the fastest darts player the world's ever seen; and I always had a soft spot for Christian Kist, who won the BDO world title back in the day

– his nickname was Lipstick. Mark Holden meanwhile was so fond of being called Top Banana that he had it tattooed on the back of his neck, which I consider reckless to say the very least, particularly as I had more time for the joint nickname he shared with his mate Paul Whitworth – they were big, bald and ballsy, they looked like the sort of guys who'd turn you away from your local nightclub for wearing trainers, and when they played together they called themselves The Bruise Brothers.

If you're open to having a laugh at your own expense, often the best nicknames are ones based on how you look. Colin Lloyd, former world number one, Grand Prix champion and World Matchplay champion – also friend, neighbour, and generally fantastic guy (because he makes me rock cakes) – ended up with the nickname Jaws based purely on a tooth configuration I can only describe as fang-esque; he smiled so wide and looked so much like a shark that he's still known as Jaws today, even after having his teeth done. Then there's Germany's René Eidams, who's called The Cube because when you actually look at him the name's not far off: five feet five inches tall and about the same distance from side to side.

But if you're trying to come up with a good nickname, I'd advise you not to go too far with physical appearances. Only Jaws can pull that off. Daryl Gurney, who's world class and in the Premier League having won two majors, has a long face with a big chin and changed his name to Super Chin. Super Chin. I'll say that a third time: *Super* Chin. He likes it and it's stuck, but my verdict is that it's childish and pathetic, and I've told him so in no uncertain terms. His management need to be taken to task over this.

There really are some truly atrocious nicknames knocking around. Some I have a problem with on a moral and ethical level. Peter Manley, for example, went by the name of One Dart – a self-given name based on the idea that he only used one dart at a double to finish. When things were going well in a match he'd hold his finger up to signify 'one', but it's rubbish because he didn't always finish on a double with one dart and you simply can't give yourself a nickname that's not true. (You might say, 'Wayne, I can't help but notice that you had 501 in your own name and didn't always hit exactly 501', to which I say these are my rules and I reserve the right to make them up as I go along.)

If I'm honest, in the realm of the darts nickname there are far more don'ts than dos. Often for very good reasons. I remember once when James Wade was thinking of changing his name to James 'The Blade' Wade and we had to point out than in today's society discussing any sort of blades throws up something questionable. As with Mr Glitter, you don't want anything that'll connect you with something negative.

It's also extremely bad form to take a shine to someone else's nickname and just decide it's yours. Boris Koltsov decided to call himself The Viking, but there was already a player called The Viking, and that was Andy Fordham, the 2004 world champion, who'd started off with The Viking, and will forever be known as The Viking. Theft is just not fair or right, and while I will concede that Vikings did historically have a habit of simply turning up and taking whatever they fancied, I feel that sort of behaviour is best left to seafaring Norsemen of the eighth century.

There are a few more examples of name appropriation: at one point both Andy and Terry Jenkins were competing, each calling himself Jenks, a rubbish name that neither of them should have been fighting over, but Andy kicked up a stink before changing his name to Rocky, on account of having been involved in the odd bar-room fracas. Then there's the strange situation of former world number one Alan 'The Iceman' Warriner, who retired and said he didn't care when Gerwyn Price took over that nickname. Thing is, Alan may not have cared but I did. And I still do. Okay, not as much as I used to. But I still care. A bit.

Laziness is another big no-no. I should preface this by saying I have no problem with simplicity – for instance, I've always quite liked The Power. (I'm not so big a fan that I'd have it tattooed up my arm, like Phil does, but it works for him and he's got the talent to back it up, which is just as well because otherwise it would just sound sarcastic.) No, the problem is the type of laziness that means darts is swarming with Barrys calling themselves Bazzer.

This just suggests lack of imagination. Even more egregiously, there's the type of nickname I've always said should be avoided – not that anyone listens to me – and that's the type that involves adding a 'y' to the end of your name. One particularly upsetting 'make an effort, mate' example comes from Mark Walsh, who's a nice guy and a decent player, but whose first attempt at a nickname was Special Brew for no reason other than that he liked drinking Special Brew.

The good news is that Walsh realised his error and changed his nickname. The bad news is that he changed it to Walshy. He sounds like a cricketer. God love my wicket-obsessed colleagues, but they've never been strong on nicknames, and Walshy is a *total* cricketer name. There are more: Anthony Fleet is Fleety, the vest-clad Dave Chisnall is Chizzy ... I'm well aware that you might find this sacrilegious, but I'd even say Barneveld being called Barney falls into this category. Sometimes you see these attempts and you just think: 'Come on now, fella. You're better than that.' No imagination, no flair, no humour, no thanks. I don't think it's too dramatic to say a poor nickname should result in a lifetime ban from all sport.

The opposite of a name that makes too much sense is one that's just confusing. For instance, my Canadian Sky Sports colleague John Part used to come on to *Star Wars* music and called himself Darth Maple. While I understand each element of his nickname I still have no idea what it's actually supposed to mean. I know Darth Vader is from *Star Wars* and I get that the maple leaf is reminiscent of Canada, but amalgamating the two doesn't work for me and never has. I just don't know what Darth Maple is supposed to mean. It's a mess. I said to him once: 'John, why are you doing this to yourself?' He just stared at me. We still sometimes debate his walk-on music and nick-name – truly ridiculous for a three-time world champion and darting legend.

While I'm thrilled when I come across nicknames that totally work (e.g. my own one), and I have a grudging admiration for the chaotic energy of nicknames like Darth Maple that don't work at all, the real danger zone, for me, is nicknames that *almost* work but don't. Anything that requires an explanation is too complicated and should be vetoed. Take Keegan

'The Needle' Brown. For this name to work you need to know (a) that Keegan's from the Isle of Wight, and (b) that the Isle of Wight boasts a tourist attraction called The Needles. Now I don't want to cause any offence here, because I'm as big a fan of freestanding chalk-based geological phenomena as the next man, but when you're competing on the world stage you need to acknowledge the limited international recognition enjoyed by a few bits of disjointed cliff.

And don't give me the 'Needle works because darts have a pointy end' argument. I am simply not having it.

Another thing to bear in mind when you're choosing a nickname is that the more imaginative the name, the more expansive your range of merchandise can be. My Hawaiian shirts may have led to my name, but it's my name that ended up shifting those thousands of shirts I kept in my garage.

Some professionals go a little too far with the merch, though, losing sight of whether or not it makes any sense in relation to their name. I suppose it's hard to see *anything* when there are pound signs in front of your eyes. But that's what leads us to the sort of situation where Jamie 'Jabba' Caven winds up selling – of all things – condoms. If memory serves they might even have had a picture of his face on them, which you'd think would be something of a mood-killer, but that didn't stop him. (I do admire the hustle, even if from a birth control angle I do have to question the wisdom of selling condoms alongside darts. Caven also sells baby bibs with his name on, and maybe that's all you need to know. Either way, he certainly loves his merch.)

The most deranged example of a nickname I've ever encountered is Dutch player Jan Dekker, who used to come on wearing a Roger Federer-style white jacket, and decided to call himself ... Mr Coat. *MR COAT!* He later changed it to Jan 'Double' Dekker, which I rather liked. Partly because it's a name that might make you think of either a two-tiered London bus, or alternatively a seminal nougat-based chocolate bar. It's multipurpose.

And that ambiguity is important, if only for legal reasons. Consider the cautionary tale of James Wilson, who now goes by the name Lethal Biscuit. Wilson had started off calling himself Jammy Dodger. The first word hinged on an excruciatingly tenuous connection to 'James', but it just about worked. I was prepared to allow it. Except, while I'm no copyright or trademark lawyer, I'd say it's always worth steering clear of Big Biscuit when you're choosing your darts name, particularly if like James Wilson you're so attached to your moniker that you go as far as to include a picture of an actual Jammy Dodger biscuit on the back of your shirt. I mean, you can hardly plead ignorance when you're dressed up as the biscuit whose name you've nicked. It was big mistake, obviously – a couple of legal letters later, Wilson ended up having to ditch Jammy Dodger altogether.

Part of me still wonders if Wilson caved too early. I mean, he would have lost eventually, but imagine what a great conversation starter it would be if you could get yourself involved in a legal feud with a biscuit. 'I hear you're moving back in with your mum?' 'Yeah, lost my house after libelling a Rich Tea.' A restraining order forbidding you to go within 200 metres of a custard cream? A suspended sentence for aggravated assault on a chocolate Hobnob? This is after-dinner speaker GOLD.

In any case, Jammy Dodger became Lethal Biscuit. I remember saying to him at the time: 'You do realise you'll have to explain this whole debacle to people every single time you mention Lethal Biscuit?'

'Oh dear,' he said, 'I didn't really think about that.'

But that's how his name stayed. (For the record, Lethal Biscuit has the same management as Super Chin. Need I say more?)

If you're reading this book there's a strong chance you may have ambitions to become a professional dartist in your own right one day, so if you would like to get in touch with me before moving forward with your new nickname I'd be happy to provide my consultancy services. I don't want it to seem like I'm self-appointed judge, jury and executioner here, but the whole nickname scene is madness, someone needs to take control of the mess and if that person is me then so be it. My fees are reasonable and my judgement is fair, but my decision is final.

3.

VENUES

During 2020, the twelve-month debacle I'll hencefor-ward refer to as The Cursed Year, we saw the sudden rise of home darts, or internet darts, or whatever you want to call it. It was an impressively speedy reaction to a relentlessly atrocious global shitshow, but as the time went by it was hard to feel that the experience wasn't slightly empty. What was missing, of course, was being in the same room as the spectators. Fans play such an important part in making this sport seem dramatic and exciting. Whether it's eight people in your local pub or eight thousand in a packed arena, you need an audience. Without it, all you've got is two people throwing metal at a wall.

Like most people my first taste of real-life darts was in the pub setting. I was born in north London and grew up in Islington, where by the age of seven I was watching my dad play in local pubs. Most often he was playing in The Clothworkers Arms on the corner of Arlington Avenue and Bevan Street, not far from Shoreditch Park.

It was a proper old-fashioned boozer and of course it's long since closed. These days the Clothworkers is … well, I'll give you three guesses. You got it in one: it's a residential build-ing. I do sometimes wonder if property developers in London couldn't have saved themselves a lot of time and hassle during the 2000s if instead of turning old banks into pubs and pubs into flats or branches of McDonald's, they'd simply turned the banks directly into flats or fast-food restaurants, cutting out the middle man and leaving the pubs alone.

Back in the eighties, though, when the Clothworkers was in its prime, that's where you'd find my dad and his mates, and round the corner from the dartboard sitting quietly with an orange squash you'd find a miniature Wayne Mardle.

It would be hard to explain to someone who's only ever known the era of gastropubs, child-friendly areas and crayons and colouring sheets on every table, but boozers of the eighties and nineties didn't exactly pride themselves on their family-friendliness or their culinary expertise – they were drinking establishments, with peanuts on the bar if you were lucky and perhaps, on a Sunday, a plate of admittedly rather tasty roast potatoes. Pubs were for hard drinking, not soft play – the near-est they got to 'child-friendly' was 'child-tolerant, as long as the kids keep quiet and out of the way'. If we behaved ourselves they'd turn a blind eye.

All of which explains me hiding round the corner, with my dad having to ask the guv'nor if it was alright for me to use the loo, but as I got a little older I started to understand more about how pubs worked. Most of all, I started to understand that this was where darts happened. And eventually I got to have my own go on the board. But in order to do that I first had to learn to mark – that's when you officiate between two other players, writing down the scores. My dad always said to me: 'You can come with me, and you can watch, but you're not going to play unless you can mark the board.' I'd learned to do that at the age of ten, and by the time I was eleven I was playing in the same team as him.

My advice here: if you're getting into darts, go to a pub. It was a great experience for me, I was under no pressure at all, and while I did get the occasional request to calm down if I was getting cocky, there was nobody telling me what I 'should' be doing. I could only have got all that down the pub or the club. The pubs and clubs were a massive learning experience for me. I learned to win but I also learned to lose, meaning that I was learning about the game but I was also learning about myself. I didn't realise it until afterwards, but those were massively important days in my life.

I never started playing competitively until we moved out to Romford. My dad used to take me down the Co-Op Club, which was a social venue for people who worked – and you've probably guessed where this one's going – for the local Co-Op. They'd have tournaments down there on a Sunday night and I'd bother my dad every single weekend: 'Come on, Dad, I really want to play.' Of course there was nobody else there my age; it was full of middle-aged men. But there was one middle-aged man in particular who caught my eye.

Looking back it's amazing that at the age of twelve I was hanging out in the same boozer as Bobby George – one of the biggest personalities in the entire history of darts. Years later his self-designed mansion would contain its own purpose-built pub, but back when I first met him his drinking establishment of choice was the Co-Op.

Bobby refused to play me, for reasons I'll explain later on in the book, but the good news is that plenty of other blokes in the Co-Op Club, and other local pubs I'd start visiting, didn't have any qualms at all about taking on a twelve-year-old, and that's how I learned the ropes. That whole experience was my darts apprenticeship: seeing what it was all about, playing darts against men who were better than me, losing every time, and then, week by week, getting the occasional win in here and there. I wanted my age to be nothing to do with it: I didn't want to be someone who was 'good for his age', I simply wanted to be a good darts player. When I was on the oche it was as if I forgot my age, and as I started beating them everyone else forgot it too. (The bar staff, sadly, never did.)

Growing up in pubs and clubs with people older than me, I didn't have those rebellious teenage years of hanging round with kids and getting led astray. By the age of fifteen I wasn't drinking crap cider in the park or looking for a nightclub to go to, I was looking for a tournament in Lincolnshire where I could win £500. By twenty, I didn't want to go to Magaluf with my friends, I wanted to go to Hemsby and win a darts event. I don't feel like I missed out on anything – in fact, that early experience of hanging out with people outside my own area of experience ended up giving me loads of self-confidence. I've walked into rooms full of people like David Beckham where I should feel totally out of my comfort zone, but somehow I feel I can make it work. A year or two ago I was at a dinner and sitting on a table with Alan Shearer, Seb Coe and Mike Tindall. Without my grounding in those pubs as a teenager I don't think I'd have been able to say a word to those legendary sportsmen. As it was, I could hold a conversation with them.

In 2021 there are fewer dartboards in pubs than ever before. From time to time there's talk in the darts world along the lines of: 'Let's get darts out of the pub.' The reasoning, I guess, is that some people feel pubs are a bad look for the sport. But no. Darts must never leave the pubs. Any attempt to pretend pubs aren't part of darts is an attempt to deny the sport its past, not to mention its present and its future.

All that being said, there comes a time for decent darts players when they outgrow the pub tournaments and find themselves on the conveyor belt to the big time. That's when the bigger clubs and conference centres enter the picture, as the lure of the World Championship grows stronger.

Even though it's no longer used for the PDC World Championship, the Circus Tavern in Purfleet, Essex, still holds a special place in the heart of many a darts fan. Now there are some beautiful spots in Essex, but I'd challenge even the most ardent Essex evangelist to suggest that the location of the Circus Tavern, just round the corner from the Purfleet bypass and nestled near local cultural hotspots such as 'the ESSO garage' and 'Purfleet Truck Wash', is ever likely to be a designated conservation area. The Tavern itself isn't even much to look at, and there's no avoiding the fact that the building doubles as a 'gentlemen's club', but surprisingly for such a modest establishment that place built an international reputation in the darts world. Fourteen World Championships took place in that unassuming building, and Phil Taylor won all but three, but by 2007 the World Championship had moved from the 1,000-capacity Tavern to the 3,500-capacity Alexandra Palace, a spectacular Grade II listed building in north London that's about as far as it's possible to get from a dilapidated strip club.

I've got mixed feelings about the move to big venues. Don't get me wrong – some of those enormous venues are amazing, and the Ahoy Arena in Rotterdam is somewhere I'd love to have played; whenever I'm there on commentating duties I get such a buzz. But while Ally Pally gives off its own kind of buzz, it's not quite the same buzz as you get from 1,200 people crammed like sardines into a sweaty room. (Not to mention the fact that if you forgot your backstage pass at the Circus Tavern you could just nip round the back and have a quiet word with security – at Ally Pally it's a twenty-minute walk to security, where you'll need photo ID, two recent utility bills and a note from your mum.)

One thing I will say for the larger venues is that the facilities are usually a lot better, and as you move up you'll get to venues that boast their own green rooms and practice rooms. Rooms where you and your family can devour freshly made vol-au-vents and drink wine until you're bandy. These days when I do commentary we go straight to the press room and that's it: we sit and look at a monitor, get our laptops out and start looking for stats, but I'll never forget the feeling of being a player at one of those big arenas – the O2, the Echo in Liverpool, the MEN in Manchester. You feel like a superstar when you get taken round the back entrance, through the stage door, and then you're led to the practice room.

In truth it doesn't take much for somewhere to qualify as a practice room: there'll be a little bar in the corner in case someone wants a beverage (which they always do), and four or five dartboards set up next to each other. You turn up, get your darts out, and crack on. And if I'm making a backstage practice room sound purpose built, don't get too excited because purpose built they most certainly are not. Quite often it'll be a disused kitchen with fridges all over the place and chest freezers stacked up in the corner. And more than once, I've found that the hospitality suite is in fact a disused squash court. Cosy. (Sidenote: I've learned the hard way that, due to unusual acoustics, farts sound really loud in a squash court.)

The main problem with those big venues is that they are, by their nature, very big. Even players who don't get regular exercise will get their steps up on days they're playing in arenas. Most of them are built like a huge ring doughnut and it's easy to get disorientated; if you're not paying attention you end up walking twice around them before you find your destination. Eventually you need to admit defeat and actually ask someone where you're supposed to be going. The main problem is that most arenas look the same when you're backstage: endless corridors with the vague smell of cleaning products, people pushing trolleys around and so on, meaning that you could be in Manchester and think you know where you're going, but only because in fact you're remembering where you'd need to go if you were in a venue that's actually in Berlin.

So it's not always glamorous. But the changing rooms? Oh, those are the ones. When it's somewhere like the O2, and you know P!nk or The Rolling Stones have been there too, it's good for the ego. One moment of superstar treatment really sticks in my mind. I was in Cologne and turned up with Phil Taylor, Raymond van Barneveld and multiple world champions. There were 17,000 people at this exhibition and each player got his own security guard. I wasn't quite sure what to do with mine, as he wasn't really one for smalltalk. Confusingly he also doubled as a runner for food and drink. My own personal killer butler.

You might wonder how a security guard, who you'd hope would be glued to their client for the entire event, can also be the person whose job it is to go and fetch food. I definitely don't remember the part in *The Bodyguard* where Kevin Costner goes off to fetch Whitney Houston a Zinger Tower meal. Perhaps in security circles it's a well-established fact that anyone likely to make an attempt on the life of a professional sportsman will do so only once the sportsman's had a nice lunch. 'Never lunge at someone with an empty stomach.' Is that on the list of dos and don'ts at assailant training school? That must surely be it – giving me a security guard/food scavenger hybrid was in no way an attempt by the organisers to keep staffing costs down and I was totally safe the entire time.

Anyway, there was a point when the staff were scurrying around desperate to help me with 'all my stuff' and I was just stood there with my darts in my pocket, ready to go. They looked quite underwhelmed – not long before we turned up, the venue had been dealing with Shania Twain and Celine Dion with their huge entourages and rider demands, and here was Wayne Mardle, shuffling around with three darts in his pocket.

But like I say, when you see the photos on the walls of these places it's nice to know you're close to greatness. I don't imagine that's a one-way thing, either. I expect it's quite natural for Beyoncé to turn up at the O2 and tell herself: 'I've finally made it. Those twenty Grammys and millions of records sold were okay, but now that I've stood on the same slightly stained industrial carpet as five-time World Championship semi-finalist Wayne Mardle I feel truly validated not only as an artist but also as a human being.'

While she's famous for 'Crazy in Love' and the nearest I've got to that is being mildly out of control in Hove, of all the big celebrities I think it's Beyoncé who's probably the one who could turn her hand to darts most effectively, with the possible exception of Dame Judi Dench. As for whether Beyoncé's a fan of the sport? Well, I'm not in a position to say. All I can say here is that if, for the sake of argument, Beyoncé and Jay-Z were regulars on the circuit it's very likely that players and commentators such as myself would be obliged to sign some sort of non-disclosure agreement forbidding us from discussing it in public. So while I'm not saying I've seen Beyoncé and Jay-Z at the PDC finals, nor am I saying I haven't. I'm simply saying, if I had, I'd likely not be able to tell you.

But I digress. The irony of darts is that the higher you go, and the further your career takes you, the less likely you are to be competing in pubs, but the more likely you are to be booked for exhibitions, which more often than not end up taking place in pubs. That's like Tom Daley getting to the very height of his sport and being booked to wow audiences in a paddling pool. Or, to use the example of Beyoncé, my biggest fan (potentially!

I cannot confirm or deny), picking up another twenty Grammys then finding herself in an *X Factor* audition room. On the plus side it means that even the world's biggest darts players are never too far away from their roots – or the fans who've supported them along the way.

Which is not to say exhibitions aren't sometimes rather … challenging. When you get out of your car in the pub carpark wearing your shorts and flip-flops, you can never be certain what the next few hours will bring. The worst place I've ever played darts was at an exhibition in Holland, and little did I know what was in store when I was dropped off by my Dutch bookings agent, Suzanne. She agreed that she'd be back to pick me up six hours later, at about 1am, then off she sped. I sometimes wonder if her swift exit was anything to do with the fact that she knew the horrors that lay in wait.

When I walked in, the place was absolutely filthy, and I immediately knew it was going to be a dismal night. Things got worse when they showed me where I'd be playing: the board was a foot too high, and there was no way to move it down. 'This,' I thought to myself, 'is going to be like Stephen Hendry turning up and playing on a kid's table.'

'We can't move it down,' they told me. 'We've tried.'

'So you know it's wrong?'

'It'll be fine.'

Reader, it was not fine. The next problem was that the floor was entirely made of quarry tile, and you don't need to be an expert in press-formed building materials to know that if a dart falls out onto a surface like that, the dart's going to come off worst. From the point, to the barrel, to the stem and the flight, there's literally no part of a dart that isn't going to be annihilated by one of those abominable clay quadrilaterals. I asked if they had any sort of rug or carpet they could put down – perhaps some plywood we could use as the oche as well. It'd be the wrong distance, but I didn't care by that point. I'd been using the same darts for twenty-five years and I wasn't about to take any risks. No, they said. They did not have any floor coverings.

By 9pm the place was getting busy but I hadn't thrown a single dart, people were starting to get moody, and the next thing I knew the landlady appeared with – and I kid you not – a duvet. A proper, kingsize 13.5-tog affair. She chucked it on the floor and told me to get on with it. And that's what the rest of the evening looked like: me playing darts in something that felt like a home furnishings warehouse, with people wandering around tripping over that bloody duvet and spilling their drinks everywhere. It was chaos from start to finish, a compete endurance test and one of my three least enjoyable evenings ever as a human being, let alone as a darts player.

(For context, the other two nights in that unholy Top 3 are the dismal evening when Tony Adams scored the winner against Tottenham Hotspur in the FA Cup semi-final in 1993, and the time I was so drunk on a stag do at Ascot races that I shat myself on the minibus on the way home.)

Things aren't always any better closer to home. A few years back I turned up at a pub in Yorkshire after a long drive and when I met the landlord I enquired where I could get changed and get ready for the show. I should have known something was up when I noticed that the supposed 'banqueting hall' I was due to play in was a draughty extension that looked like it was due for demolition, but then I was told where I'd be getting ready: 'The toilets.'

This isn't actually uncommon, and I'm not one for airs and graces so I'm fine getting changed in a toilet cubicle, but what greeted me that day was an uncommonly bleak tableau. The Saturday crowd had just left the pub, and the floor of the toilet was covered in some sort of liquid. In fact I would go so far as to say it was – and this is a word I so rarely have an opportunity to deploy in everyday life, and where better than a future best-seller – AWASH. Awash with what? Hard to say, but as a betting man I'd be foolish to wager against there being a high proportion of piss in the room that day. I did note a leaking cistern which gave me some hope that the lake of mystery excreta was only partly disgusting as opposed to 100 per cent disgusting, but either way the floor was wet and, as there was apparently nowhere else for me to get changed, quite soon so were my socks and trousers.

By the time I emerged, ready to turn on the old Mardle razzle dazzle and give a pub full of darts fans a night they'd never forget, I was soaking wet and stinking of toilet. I was the night's star attraction and I spent the whole thing potentially – in fact quite probably – covered in the piss of countless men. It's times like that when the mind rather wanders, in this instance to the topic of which is the least glamorous: to be covered in someone else's piss, or to be covered in your own. If it's your own, that means you've pissed yourself, and that's rarely a good look, even if does usually mean that you've had some fun in the preceding hours. But someone else's piss, or the piss of many others, has to be worse. I consoled myself by saying it could have been worse than urine, but you know you're having a bad night when the best you can tell yourself is: 'At least it's not human shit.'

As darts has risen in stature, that sort of debacle is less and less common. In fact, I can't remember the last time I got asked to change in a toilet, leaky or otherwise, and that's one of the definite upsides of darts gradually becoming bigger and more highly regarded. It's strange to think I might be a member of the last generation of darts players to endure all that, and I certainly wouldn't expect Michael van Gerwen to be getting changed in a pissy toilet. I expect he'd react with an 'Are you kidding me?', or some rather less polite Dutch variant.

The Dutch Variant sounds like a Matt Damon espionage thriller, doesn't it? I might see if it's available on Amazon Prime Video.

4.

AMATEUR TO PRO

Due to a surprising number of local councils' inexplicable nervousness regarding children throwing sharpened objects at each other in school playgrounds, aka health and safety gone mad, there's no straightforward equivalent to jumpers for goalposts in the world of darts. Playing darts means using darts and a dartboard. The good news, therefore, is that if you're showing an early interest in throwing, it's pretty likely that the equipment you start out with won't be far off the equipment you could end up using on the professional circuit.

I've discussed equipment already, but for the avoidance of doubt a Winmau or Unicorn board from Argos, and a £15 set of tungstens, will set you up just fine. Don't be sidetracked by the dazzling array of electronic scoreboards, grip wax, darts chalk and paraphernalia. Your local sports shop will be more than happy to load you up with as much as you can carry, but at the end of the day, or at least at the end of your first day, all you need is something to throw, and something to throw it at.

So let's say you've got your kit home on Saturday afternoon and your dad's spent half an hour making a right state of your bedroom wall by using the wrong drill bit on masonry, but finally the board's up and ready to accept some tungsten into its welcoming sisaly body. What next? What do you do in the coming weeks, months and years to stand the best chance of one day battling it out against someone like Barney, enjoying the glory of life as an international darting superstar, or maybe even achieving the ultimate sporting dream: becoming the next Wayne Mardle?

Brace yourself, because it's actually the next sixty seconds that matter most. Every single player from Phil Taylor to Fallon Sherrock will have started off doing exactly what you will now be doing: quite simply, throwing at a board in a way that feels comfortable.

You pick up the dart in a way that seems natural to you, and you throw it with no thought about aiming. If it still feels comfortable after two minutes, carry on. If not, shift your stance and try for another two minutes. Even if it takes a couple of attempts, you'll find your action. You'll practise for years to come, but this first session in front of the board is the most important day of your darting career: it sets in stone the action you'll stay with forever, and that'll decide whether you're a future winner or a future loser. However much you refine it in the coming years this will always fundamentally be how you play. So while I'm inviting you to be as relaxed as possible in this moment, don't underestimate its importance. With those first few darts you could be setting a precedent for how you're going to throw forevermore.

One tip here: after those first few throws, try to figure out how you can reduce any possible variation in your movement.

The aim in a good stance is that you'll be able to recreate it again, and again, and again. John Henderson stands at the board and literally rocks back and forth on his feet. It's so noticeable that he even comes on to Status Quo's 'Rockin' All Over the World'. He moves from his front foot to his back foot before he throws, meaning that the timing of his release has to be perfectly calculated to match a specific point in a rock. He's a world-class operator but if he didn't have that rock, which introduces an unnecessary variable to his throw, he'd have more control. The irony, however, is that if he did stop now he'd actually be worse, because he doesn't know how to throw *without* that rock. If you took away his rock he'd be a worse darts player; but if he'd taken it away thirty years ago, who knows how much better he might have been today? (Rhetorical question – *I* know, and he would have been at least 30 per cent better.)

There have been some right shockers out there, and they've done inexplicably well. Kevin McDine throws darts from about a foot to the right-hand side of his head with his elbow pointing inwards – an appalling and disgusting way to throw, which nonetheless works for him. When I first saw his action it was grimly mesmerising, in much the same way that bar brawls, people falling into holes and the 2019 movie version of *Cats* are all mysteriously magnetic. It's hard to look away when Kevin's throwing. I remember being interviewed on live TV once, after I'd played against Kevin and his ludicrous technique. The game hadn't gone well. 'I can't believe I lost to someone with such a rubbish action,' I said. You probably think I was being overly brutal and you're right. Improbably, he made the semi-final of the Grand Slam of Darts.

To my mind the best player with the worst technique (and it really is an abysmal technique) is Serbian dartslinger Mensur Suljović. He lifts the back leg; he's constantly leaning then not leaning; he jumps with the right foot and lifts the heel. It's more like watching an Olympic gymnast than a world-class darts player, and he needs to replicate this ludicrous display every single time he throws a dart. An impossibility for most players, but Suljović pulls it off, again and again.

It's staggering, and not a little horrifying. He releases the dart late, he releases the dart early; he throws hard, he throws soft; he's lunging at the board ... and they're still going in the treble 20s. Despite everything, at the point of release he's as perfect as anyone. Almost every other darts professional I know has a single technique and Suljović has about a hundred. It's a mess, but for that reason he's rather magical to watch throwing. Just don't get any ideas.

I was lucky to develop my own style early on, and it proved very effective very quickly. I'd never set out thinking I was on the road to being a professional, just like you don't think of World Cup glory the first time you kick a football, but before long I was starting to beat people in the local pubs, and I felt like fate was pulling me forwards, dragging me in the direction of my darting destiny.

If beating some fellas in a boozer sounds easy, you'd be surprised how tricky it can be. The atmosphere was always jovial and fun – a load of people having a good time – until the latter stages of a tournament, where things would inevitably turn serious. Particularly in the eyes of a certain few players. It took me a while to realise this, but if there were seventy or so people in a pub for a tournament, sixty of them would be there for a night out, five would be there for a nice old competitive game of darts and to see if they could perhaps nick a couple of quid, and the remaining five were there to win, and *only* to win. I learned to spot the ringers a mile off. It wasn't hard: they were there alone, having driven from God-knows-where for no reason other than to thrash a room full of strangers, and they didn't mix, socialise or have fun. I used to watch them like a hawk.

Not that I was entirely innocent when it came to the concept of looking further afield for a good game, although when I moved on to the Double Top – a venue as famous as any darts pub ever has been (in Essex) – it was because I was looking for a new challenge. I wanted to get better at my game, and I knew I'd only do that by playing against better players.

And I did improve. In fact, the Double Top was the location of my first ever tournament win, on my thirteenth birthday in 1986. I played a chap called Tommy Wilson in the final. He'd played for London and Essex and was forever in finals and semi-finals of open events around the country. The prize that day was £50 to the winner, and precisely £0 to the runner-up. In situations like that the done thing is to agree that whoever wins will split the top prize with whoever comes second, so that day it would have been £30 for the winner and £20 to the runner-up. But it was clear to me that Tommy would not be giving £20 to someone who'd been thirteen for less than twenty-four hours, so I made the decision that I'd take the same winner-takes-all approach, and keep the full prize if I won.

Well, I did win. I beat Wilson 3–0. I was better than him on that particular day, and that was that. I was better than *anyone* that day. I thought I was going to be given a £50 note, but instead I was given three £10 notes by my dad, who'd been handed the prize money and had immediately given £20 to Tommy Wilson.

'We agreed to split,' Tommy shrugged.

I wasn't having that. 'No, we didn't,' I fired back.

Tommy looked shiftily to my dad, who said: 'Er, yes we did.'

Cheers, Dad, for that vote of confidence! Tommy and my dad had made the agreement earlier in the day – my dad had wanted to make sure I went away with a bit of cash for coming second. On one hand I was disappointed my dad hadn't thought I could win. On the other hand, he'd clearly felt I could get all the way to the final, and Tommy was a worthy opponent, so I didn't feel too bad. In any case I didn't have time to consider the finer points of our father/son dynamic because I was too busy being furious about being ripped off to the tune of twenty quid. Thirty quid was still a decent amount of money to a thirteen-year-old back in 1986, but fifty would have got me a portable telly from Argos. A black-and-white one, to be fair, but still. I was fuming. Tommy Wilson still reminds me of that story: 'Do you remember when I nicked twenty quid off you?' Oh yes, Tommy, I remember.

One key part of your journey from amateur to pro will be finding the time – and the drive – to fit darts in around everything else that's happening in your life. That means navigating the demands of those 'proper jobs' nearly every professional has used to pay the bills on their way to the top.

Bobby George worked as a nightclub bouncer, Fallon Sherrock was a hairdresser and, quite wonderfully, Phil Taylor made ceramic toilet-roll handles. As for me, when I left school at fifteen I found work with a company called Nevill Long, who sold the sort of suspended ceilings you find in offices where management clearly feel regular ceilings would give employees just a little too much vertical space.

I'd been hurled into the world of work with no qualifications to my name, but a mate I played darts with had got me in the door at Nevill Long and I took the position of warehouseman. That means I learned to drive a forklift. (An important life skill and you'll never know when you might need it, although I've literally never needed it, but if the moment comes at least I'm ready.) In hindsight I shouldn't have been in such a dangerous environment at that age and I should absolutely not have been cavorting around a warehouse on a motorised lifting vehicle, but fortunately I already looked twenty at that point, and nobody ever questioned my presence.

Not something a company could get away with in 2021 and quite possibly legally murky even then, but like non-existent seatbelts and the ability to buy single fags from the ice-cream van parked outside your school it was acceptable in the eighties, and anyway it put some money in my pocket.

Not, however, quite as much money as I might have liked. After a few months on the job my warehouse mates Steve and Martin agreed that we should be getting more in our pay packets each week, but our attempts at negotiation didn't go very well. We made a pact that we'd approach the boss collectively and put on a united front, reasoning that he couldn't say no to all three of us. In any case, we only wanted an extra twenty quid a week each. (Twenty quid being an important figure for me: it was what I was paying my mum each week for housekeeping.) So the three of us climbed up the steel staircase to the boss's office and knocked on the door. Those negotiations in full:

Boss: 'What can I do for you fellows?'

Martin: 'We haven't had a raise in a while, can we have an extra twenty quid a week?'

Boss: 'You're all sacked.'

He told us to get out and that was that. In all honesty getting up at 6am every day was not for me, but instant dismissal really wasn't the outcome I'd been hoping for.

Still, that left me with extra time to play darts, although that peace and quiet wouldn't last long. The government's YTS initiative and a drive aimed at increasing teens' 'vocational prospects' ended up getting me a job interview with the Association of Accounting Technicians, a professional body with thousands of accountants as members. I got the job. The commute was a total pain. Each morning I'd walk to the bus stop, wait for a bus from Romford Greyhound Stadium to Romford station, get a train to Liverpool Street, then a tube to Farringdon, and finally I'd walk to the office. At the end of the day I'd do the entire thing in reverse. The daily traipse to and from work was nearly a full-time job in itself.

Thrilling it was not, but I joined the company at sixteen believing I'd be some sort of trainee accountant, so it seemed like a good start. But my role ended up being that of the office manager, looking after internal audits, invoices and general nonsense.

I hope I'm not doing my former employer a disservice here when I say that in my heart of hearts I was more passionate about darts than I was about bulk-buying Biros or sniffing out the most likely culprit in the notorious Communal Fridge Milk Disappearance manhunt of 1996. By nineteen the darting side of my double life had taken over, and some weeks I was earning more on the oche than I was during office hours. I was winning £500 here, £700 there; one tournament in Yarmouth got me £1,000.

In your own journey from amateur to pro you'll reach a point where you're faced with a dilemma. There's no knowing when the point will come, but the question will always be the same: do you carry on as you are, working nine to five in your regular job and keeping darts on the side, or do you take a leap of faith? Some people never do take the leap. I've seen players far better than me unable to go professional (thank Christ); others just have to wait for the right time.

For me the circumstances weren't there until 2002 – I'd been working at the AAT for over a decade by that point, slowly building up my game on weekends. Until 2002 I didn't feel stable financially, and whenever I considered turning pro the timing just seemed *off*. But one day it was as if the planets were beginning to align.

Most importantly I needed a plan, and in 2002 I sat down with my wife Donna, who you'll be hearing a lot about in this book, and we did the sums together. Maybe thirteen years hanging around accountants has rubbed off on me. By this point I was already taking part in exhibitions every other weekend, and I figured that if I gave up my job I'd be able to travel further for exhibitions, widening my net and allowing me to take part in even more. The exhibitions, we calculated, could pay the mortgage.

We looked at what else I could potentially win having turned pro, and figured that if things went well enough we could reach the next milestone: the point where Donna, who'd been working as a tax inspector for the Inland Revenue and wasn't enjoying it, could pack up work. I couldn't drive, so I'd have been needing to pay a driver most weekends anyway, and if Donna took on that role she could work as my driver and personal assistant, so we could make it work.

The big question was how much I could win – and that depended on which existing professionals I'd be able to beat. I remember looking at the top players in the world on the ranking list, crossing them off one by one: 'Better than them … Better than them … Beat *them* last month …' These were big names like Peter Manley and Colin Lloyd, and I felt confident I could take them on. I did end up beating all of them (even if in fairness they each got their own back), so I was right. There was only one player whose name I didn't cross off the list and that was Phil Taylor, so I was right about that too. You win some, you lose some; just try to win more than you lose.

Eventually the time came for me to hand in my notice at work. First off, I told my colleague and mate Jamie. It was a Monday, and I just came out with it. It was like telling someone a relationship was over. 'I knew this day was coming,' he sighed. 'But you've got to go, haven't you?' The news spread and everyone was giving me hugs, but I still hadn't told Gary, my boss. It didn't feel right to tell him on a Monday, but by later in the week I'd plucked up the courage to stick my head round his door.

'Gary,' I asked, 'can I have a word?'

'You're leaving, aren't you?' he replied. 'This has been coming for months.'

I'd imagined that going pro would be a transcendental moment in which clouds parted and celestial choirs rang out. In practice my transition was as mundane as one short conversation in that doorway of my boss's office. Gary couldn't have been more kind about the whole situation: I worked two weeks' notice, and that was that. I left on 13 May 2002 on a sunny day that saw the office close early so we could head to a local Farringdon pub for my leaving do. It was emotional. 'I know you're leaving for good,' Gary said that day, 'but as far as the company's concerned, we're going to think of it as a year's sabbatical. If you want to come back in twelve months, your job's still here.'

It was a thoughtful safety net, but I didn't need it. I wouldn't be going back.

I hit the ground running, playing my first event as a darts professional less than twenty-four hours after my leaving do, and in tournaments I quickly found that I was getting straight through to the finals. Sponsors, who hadn't been around before, came on board. Exhibition bookings started flooding in. By June I realised I was going to make two years' worth of money from my old job in less than six months as a darts pro. I informed Donna one morning, and by the afternoon she'd handed in her own notice. I'd achieved my goal. I was finally, unequivocally, a darts pro, and I'd made it happen myself.

5.

PDC, BDO, PDPA, DRA, WDF, WTF

I f you're new to darts and aren't yet intimately acquainted
with terms like DRA, PDPA and PDC ... Well, I rather envy
you to be honest. But if you're planning on taking your darting
forward, or even if you're simply wanting this book to make a
bit more sense, I suppose I should EWTAA (explain what those
acronyms are) and give some background on who's who, what's
what and why you need to know.

First off: the British Darts Organisation. The BDO was
founded in the early 1970s in the front room of Olly Croft, who
did a huge amount over the years to raise the profile of the sport
both in the UK and on an international level. I started playing
for London Youth in 1984 when I was eleven, then went from
youth to super league, to county, to international, and I did it
all through the BDO system.

By the late eighties, however, the world of professional
darts was going through some turbulence: there had once been
twelve televised events annually, but in the space of a couple
of years a number of sponsors walked away from the sport
and those televised events dropped from twelve to just two.

The sport wasn't growing any more; in fact, it was shrinking, and the professionals were struggling to find anywhere to play. There was turmoil, squabbling, and trouble in the ranks.

Considering the BDO had only managed to create such an impressive space for itself because of the complacency of its predecessor, the National Darts Association of Great Britain, which itself had usurped the National Darts Association, you might have thought the BDO would have been more careful about making sure its own position wasn't later challenged by another organisation. And if you did think that, you'd have been wrong.

Players and managers started talking about the dire situation with Olly Croft, making it very clear to Olly that something needed to be done. Olly, bless him, was doing his best to get things back on track, but he couldn't sort out the problem quickly enough for the players or their managers. In response, a number of those managers broke away from the BDO and in 1992 formed the World Darts Council (WDC), whose name lasted a few years before it restructured and became the Professional Darts Corporation – the PDC.

When the PDC was formed, the professionals in the BDO pretty much all walked away, leaving the BDO in a hell of a state. It never really recovered. And to say the split was acrimonious doesn't even begin to describe the day-to-day drama. The rivalry between the BDO and the PDC was instantaneous: as a BDO player I'd turn up to a neutral event like an open and I'd be told I simply couldn't play against a PDC player. If I did, the BDO would ban me. You'd go out for a friendly game of darts and it would turn into an argument. International players were turning up for multi-stage events and being told they couldn't play against their next opponent, having already got through six rounds. They'd have to forfeit the game, or be banned from all future events. It was utterly ridiculous.

For me, the breaking point came when I wanted to go to a Bob Anderson exhibition in the early 2000s. I've always liked Bob, both as a human and as a player. But when I got to the door, and because I was already a face in the BDO system, I was told by the organiser that I should reconsider coming in. Basically, if I'd gone in and even *watched* a player from the PDC, the BDO would have banned me. (Many players were indeed banned from playing in the BDO for similar things.) The whole situation was pathetic and laughable, although as I stood in the doorway that day I wasn't laughing. I was furious. I'd already been thinking of joining the PDC anyway – unlike the BDO they were clearly going in the right direction, and that's where the money was. I'd been needing a push, and the situation at that Bob Anderson exhibition was more like a shove. When I walked away from the doors of the exhibition, in my mind I was also walking away from the BDO.

The BDO ceased trading in the autumn of 2020, while I was writing this book. Despite my grievances with the organisations back in the day, it was undoubtedly a sad day for darts because amateurs desperately need a world organisation. This may well fall to the WDF (World Darts Federation), a decent operation and the great new hope for amateur darts. I do hope the WDF step up and make the most of this opportunity: it's no exaggeration to say darts, to an extent, is relying on them.

In my eyes the BDO collapsed in on itself the day Raymond van Barneveld joined the PDC in 2006: until then there'd been a chance, I guess, that the BDO could have staged some sort of comeback. But Barney's arrival at the PDC meant it now had all the best players, barring Martin Adams, and there was no doubt any more that the PDC was simply *the* place to play darts.

These days if I were to compare the the PDC to anything it would be something like Thor from the Marvel movies: a lean, well-looked-after machine, effortlessly repelling any missile thrown its way, negotiating any obstacle and powering its way through. The BDO just makes me think of the captain of a sinking vessel, leaning over the side and frantically shovelling water *into* the ship. The BDO have been the masters of their own demise. They were such an important figure in the world of darts and they squandered everything: the last BDO World Championship was a farce and only served to make the PDC seem even stronger.

The next big darts body you need to know about is the Professional Dart Players Association. It's supposedly there to act in the interests of darts professionals – its set-up is that since the early 1980s half a dozen current professionals have been elected to the PDPA board annually, and membership is open to anyone who's earned (and paid for) a PDC tour card. It's the nearest darts professionals have to a union, and members can expect to put 2 per cent of their winnings back into the PDPA in exchange for various benefits. (It used to be 3 per cent.) A decent idea, but in terms of effectiveness it's far from perfect.

My assessment of the PDPA is that it's useful, in the sense that anything slightly better than useless is by definition useful, if only slightly. These days the PDPA are definitely more help-ful to players than they've been in the past, but I still think they should look after their players better. Their responsibility has never been greater, particularly in the post-COVID era when so many low-ranking players are still recovering from having seen entire livelihoods wiped out for the best part of a year, and the PDPA really need to step up and deliver for the players who've kept them afloat for the last forty years.

The tale of poor old Erik Clarys shows just how useless the PDPA have been in the past. Back in 2006 Erik fell off a ladder while he was working and broke his elbow, leading to more than ten operations and, as you might expect, a sudden and very reluctant early retirement. He could never play again. The 3 per cent of their winnings that players give to the PDPA goes into a fund that's supposed to help out the association's members when it comes to things like healthcare, but guess how much money Erik received from the PDPA?

None. Faced with a grim period until he got back on his feet, and with his darting career in ruins, he asked if he could take back the 3 per cent he'd contributed over the years. That was declined. The reasoning, I believe, was that the PDPA thought this would lead to abuse of the system. The logic was that if they helped out Erik, *anyone* could say they had an injury and ask for their money back. There was no doubt Erik's injury was real – there was a massive scar running from his shoulder to his wrist, and that should have been evidence enough that he couldn't play any more. I found that episode quite unsettling, to be honest. It was a good few years ago now, and I know I'm not the only one in darts circles who still hasn't forgotten.

The next organisation you need to know about is the Darts Regulation Authority – the DRA – which is the sport's governing body and is concerned with administering rules and regulations, as well as establishing standards of expected behaviour and looking into the conduct of players. They're affiliated with a number of other organisations including the PDC and PDPA (as well as the DPNZ, CDC, JDC and UDUK, but let's not get into those now) which means in darting circles, and I don't want to baffle you with complicated darting terminology, the DRA basically do what they like and bloody well like what they do.

The DRA absolutely calls the shots. One side of me is thrilled that darts has cleaned up its act so much over the last few years, and I have no doubt that the DRA have been instrumental in driving this change. The other side of me finds them ridiculous. If they want to fine a player for bringing the game into disrepute – and that's *always* open to interpretation, which I'll come to shortly – the player has to fight them. The PDPA, who could step in, usually keep well out of it. And if you want to appeal a £500 fine, the fee is £800. You can imagine how the conversation goes.

DRA: 'We're fining you £500.'

Player: 'I want to appeal!'

DRA: 'Appealing costs £800.'

Player: 'The cost of appealing a £500 fine is £300 more than just paying the fine?'

DRA: 'That's right. Would you still like to appeal?'

Player: 'Er …'

DRA: 'Happy to help!!!'

And that £800 is just the tip of the iceberg. All in, the process of appealing can end up costing you £3k, so even if you get out of the fine you're still £2,500 in the hole. Given that most players don't have money to throw away like that, the DRA are in a position where it feels like they do what they like.

Least surprising revelation in this entire book: I've had quite a few run-ins with the DRA over the years. For example, in darts there's an agreement that if you lose, you stay by the board and officiate the next game. In an industry so reliant on hierarchy it's a great leveller – whether you've just turned pro or you're Raymond van Barneveld, you take your defeat and you stick around and do your duty. I like the *idea* of it and I nearly always did my bit, but to be absolutely frank with you there were times when I just couldn't stomach it: I'd lost, I felt completely rubbish, I wanted no part in it and I just needed to clear off and lick my wounds. So when those moments came along, I used to offer someone else £10 to officiate in my place. I'd lose, get the hump, give someone else ten quid and go home.

On one particular occasion, this was called out by the tournament's director, Tommy Cox. 'Wayne, bad luck today but you need to mark the board for the next game,' he said.

'Don't worry, I'll get someone to do it for me,' I replied.

'No,' he shot back. 'You need to do it yourself.'

'No I don't.'

I don't come out of this covered in glory, I'm afraid: a small argument ensued and I ended up basically telling Cox to fuck off. I mean, I say 'basically': I literally told him to fuck off. Then I fucked off myself, and let someone else mark the next game.

Inevitably the DRA found out about this little exchange, and hit me with a £50 fine. That seemed reasonable – I'm not sure if you've ever had the satisfaction of telling someone to fuck off in an argument but it's got to be worth £50 of anyone's money. Unfortunately I'd recently moved house and hadn't updated my address on the DRA database. It hadn't been intentional, although a therapist would probably tell me my unconscious simply didn't want them to know where I lived. Anyway the DRA's initial demand for £50 went to my old address, as did three reminders, and the fine doubled each time it went unpaid. By the time they eventually got in touch with me it was standing at £400. Although I have to say, it was still worth it.

One example of extreme numptyism on the part of the DRA, when I really hadn't done what I'd been accused of, and they wouldn't see sense, was the time I got whacked with a fine for not getting drunk. Just to reiterate, that's not *getting* drunk, it's *not* getting drunk.

There was a darts event. The full details of the event itself remain classified (translation: I can't remember what it was), but the drinks afterwards, held in a hotel bar, are where everything went down. Or, according to one outraged onlooker, went down then came back up again. I was standing at the bar with Kevin Painter and Andy Jenkins and there was some minor rowdiness happening. Were we paralytic? No. Had we consumed one or two bevvies? Perhaps. But our high spirits were nothing worse than you'd usually see on a weekend in any number of bars up and down the country. Key point: nobody had asked us to be quiet.

Events took a turn when one of the group decided to buy a round of Jägermeisters which, well, let's just say Jägermeister is not for me, and while it hits the spot for some, as far as I'm concerned it might as well come into existence having been squeezed directly from Satan's bumhole. I vividly remember the way it all played out: I kept refusing the Jägermeister but I was bought one anyway, so I went through the motions of downing it just to keep people happy, then turned away and spat it back into the glass. Clearly this manoeuvre wasn't likely to win any awards for etiquette, but I was as subtle as I could have been in the circumstances, and my actions were prompted by what I still consider to be two highly admirable qualities: my desire not to get shouting-on-tables drunk, and my desire not to disappoint my friends. As far as I'm concerned I should at least have got an MBE for my efforts that evening.

Instead I got a letter through the door from the DRA, informing me that I'd apparently brought the hotel – and the magnificent sport of darts – into disrepute. Now, I've heard stories about some of the things people get up to in hotels, and I can tell you this: depositing a shot glass of regurgitated beverage on the bar doesn't even touch the sides. The DRA just weren't having it. Apparently a hotel guest had moaned to the people on reception that they'd seen a man (could have been anyone) in a Hawaiian shirt (perhaps not) being sick at the bar. My actions were disgusting, apparently, and I was to be fined £700.

SEVEN HUNDRED QUID!

Given the sartorial detail noted in the complaint I couldn't really claim mistaken identity. But I personally appealed. There was a hearing and everything. The whole episode was ridiculous. Beforehand Peter Manley, there in his capacity as PDPA chairman, asked if I'd like him to sit in on my hearing to help out, but I knew he'd recently sat in on a hearing for Andy

Jenkins and his presence in the room had somehow resulted in the fine actually going *up* by a hundred quid, so I politely declined and went in alone.

There were four people sitting in the room, and they read out various statements to me. The discussion did not go well.

'You were sick.'

'I wasn't.'

'This says you were.'

'It's wrong.'

We went round and round in circles. It's funny what you remember in moments like that, but my main memory is of how the meeting ended. In the middle of negotiations I stood up, made a grand declaration – 'You're now calling me a liar, this is a kangaroo court, I want no part of it' – and walked out. I ended up paying £750.

That's not even the most absurd fine I've come across. That dubious honour falls to the penalty the DRA handed to the Northern Irish player Mickey Mansell. In the DRA's eyes, Mickey made the grave and unforgivable mistake of being seen to not be playing to the best of his ability. In other words, it was a 'must try harder' fine. The only possible scenario in which that fine would make sense is if the DRA had suspected that Mickey's performance was linked to some sort of betting syndicate or match-throwing activity; in reality nothing of the sort had taken place and poor bloody Mickey ended up with a fine for ... for what? Having a bad day?

The problem is, the DRA have you over a barrel because if you don't pay the fines by a certain date, they can ban you. And in both my own case and Mickey's, we weren't big enough to stand up to that threat. If it had been Phil Taylor, who was a big pull for the entire darts industry, he'd have been able to push back, knowing that his being kicked out of darts would have been a disaster for the game. I didn't have that clout, neither did Mickey, so we paid our fines and got on with our lives.

It's easy to look back on some of my antics over the years and feel silly or that I might do things differently if given another chance, but as I've grown older I've changed, and I'm probably a better person than I was back in the day. The DRA's involvement in my personal development is approximately sod all, I should add.

In fact when it comes to darts organisations, associations, bodies and groups, the only thing I'd potentially change is the period in the early 2000s when, perhaps, I should have joined the PDC earlier than I did. As it was, I waited until 2002. Between 2000 and 2006 I was one of the world's best players, day in, day out. I had off days – we all do – but in general I was a likely runner for every single event I took part in.

Couple that with the fact that the PDC was still pretty weak between 2000 and 2002, and those two years I stayed on in the BDO could have been years in which, with the wind behind me, I might have taken a world title. Maybe I wasted a little time during my prime; maybe I missed that opportunity. But that's probably the only regret in my darting life, and in a career spanning as many years as mine I reckon that's PGG. (Pretty good going.)

6.

SUPERSTITIONS

I'll start this chapter by inviting you to sit down, if you're not already seated, to take several deep breaths and to seek a sense of inner calm. To those of a nervous disposition, anybody with existing heart problems or respiratory issues, and any reader who's recently eaten, I'd advise skipping this chapter. And now I've put in place the appropriate health and safety measures, I need to tell you about my underpants.

My blue underpants, to be specific. I'm not a superstitious person at all – I don't believe in ghosts and I barely even believe in goats. But those fantastic, lucky blue underpants made me comfortable in ways far beyond the serving suggestion depicted on their packaging: for me, the comfort wasn't just physical, but psychological too.

I'm not entirely sure how the whole thing began, but I do know that one day I realised, apropos of nothing, that every time I went away or competed, I'd need to be wearing a very specific pair of undercrackers. It had been a wild and dramatic journey through the pantheon of undergarment offerings before I settled on those perfect pants. I'd tried boxer shorts: they'd ride up. Cheap Y-fronts: that was a big no. In the end my *caleçon de choix* ended up being manufactured by Sloggi.

Back in the nineties the doomed TV channel L!ve TV, a broadcasting endeavour whose management team probably outnumbered its viewers, had a rather questionable late-night show called *Topless Darts*. It was invented by Nick Ferrari, these days best known for interviewing prime ministers on LBC, and I bring this up now because I still believe it's a real shame they never followed it up with bottomless, or at least trouserless darts. I could have cleaned up on Sloggi sponsorship back then, and I have to say that if the bigwigs at Sloggi, Armani, Calvin Klein or any other pant behemoths are reading this I'm still open to discussions.

Anyway, Sloggi are a brand well known for what we might call 'keeping everything in the right place', but it wasn't just my personal equipment that benefited from the support of these blue wonders. (By personal equipment I mean my penis, and two testicles.) Far more importantly, my game was supported too, or so I believed.

It did become a bit of an obsession. At one point I had twenty-one identical pairs of blue pants – and I appreciate you'll be wondering how it's possible to require so many when laundry's done weekly, but I needed a stockpile for those times when I'd be away in Vegas for three weeks at a time and, besides, the more pairs of pants I owned, the luckier I felt.

Then one day at the Circus Tavern I found myself playing against Colin Lloyd in the World Championship. I was feeling absolutely dreadful that day: so ill, in fact, and so sure that I was about to lose my lunch from one end or the other, that during the break – bearing in mind I don't often go off for breaks – I went outside, round the back of the Circus Tavern, took my shirt off, and lay on the wet tarmac of the carpark. (If you're concerned that this story is going to end with me soiling myself, you're safe to carry on reading. If you do specifically want to read about me soiling myself, why not turn back and revisit the Venues chapter?)

Anyway, it was always like a furnace in the Tavern – the ceilings feel about nine feet high and when you're on a stage you can more or less touch the sweaty ceiling – so I de-robed, lay down in the carpark for a few minutes during the break, then went back on stage and somehow won the game.

How amazing it was, I thought, that my lucky pants had saved the day yet again. Except when I got home that night and took my trousers off I realised I'd been wearing black pants. I was horrified and confused – a reaction I've grown accustomed to when removing my trousers, but only from other people. I realised that I must have made the error in my under-the-weather state that day, getting dressed in the darkness of that cold January morning. But the point is, I'd won an amazing game of darts without my blue pants. My first thought was: 'Who cares about the blue pants any more?' (My second thought: 'I've just been given another twenty pairs for Christmas, I hope they kept the receipt.')

From that day onwards my pants ceased to be lucky. I could no longer identify any correlation between drawers and darts performance. I wore blue pants, I wore black pants – if I was feeling particularly confident I even wore white pants. Maybe there never *had* been a correlation. Either way the magic spell was broken, and the closest I've come to a full-on superstition disappeared into thin air. (I don't even wear Sloggi any more – they stopped manufacturing that particular fit so I moved on to another brand. There's a lesson for you: don't mess with the design classics.)

That was my only real foray into the world of superstitions, but the second cousin twice removed of the superstition is the *ritual*. You'll find more rituals in the sport world than in any other industry, and darts is hardly exempt. As performers we need to feel mentally ready before a game, but there's also the fact that, win or lose, *after* a game we need to have a reason we've won, or a reason we've lost. Logically the answer is usually just a matter of 'I played better or worse today than I did on other days', but that's not useful because we're always looking ahead to our next game, and if we've done badly, telling ourselves we simply need to do better next time isn't helpful. Most of all we need a reason that isn't something to do with *us* – or the fact that we'd been drinking for four hours. No, it couldn't possibly be the five pints. Don't be so ridiculous. It must be something ... in the ether!

And so, in search of meaning and explanation, rituals develop. Many players will always demand the same afternoon meal on the day of a big game – some, for instance, will only eat Nando's. Others feel that because they didn't eat at the venue on the day of a major victory, they shouldn't eat at venues at all. I was one of those players for a while: I'd arrive four hours early, but I simply would not eat. Which is not a criticism of the catering available at those venues – although in fairness the food on offer at darting events can often spend rather a long time sitting around in hot rooms, so in one or two specific cases I do feel my stance on venue food probably saved me from some rather unfortunate incidents.

The no-food rule did, unfortunately, allow other players to exploit my rumbling tummy. I was playing James Wade in a Premier League match a few years back, and it got to the point where we were the next game on. With ten minutes to go I looked across the green room and couldn't believe my eyes: there, tucking into a massive double cheeseburger, was my opponent. Now, clearly darts isn't exactly the 100-metre sprint at the Olympics and someone's play isn't going to be overly affected by a pile of Ronald McDonald's finest, but it's still very strange and slightly shocking to see a sportsman of any sort stuffing down a double cheeseburger ten minutes before showtime.

It put me on a bit of a wobble, and the sight of James merrily chomping his way through that heap of food told me something that really upset me. Namely: he wasn't nervous. He felt totally comfortable. Darts is all about rhythm, timing and finesse in your fingertips; you can't have that with fat, grease and slices of gherkin all over the place. Well, I couldn't, anyway. But James was so nonchalant.

I saw him and I thought: 'You think you're going to win.' It's actually the perfect psychological trick to play on someone backstage. It rattled me so much. And with good reason: he absolutely annihilated me in front of eight thousand people, and another million live on *Sky Sports*.

When it comes to the stage, even getting there can become its own kind of ritual. After a while you know that the crowd expects a certain thing from each of the players – fans come to expect a specific type of energy. Even if that energy is ... no energy. Raymond van Barneveld, for instance, has to keep it cool. He *has* to. He's said before that he just can't do what I did, leaping about the place like a goat on ecstasy. Thing is, I couldn't have done what he does either. He keeps his heart rate down, but with me it was all about the ritual of knowing the audience expected something big. They expected that when I was about to appear, the show would really start.

Now, we're not robots. There were times when I just didn't feel like it. There were times when I'd say to Donna: 'Do you know what, I just don't fancy this.' But I knew the crowd expected it of me, and that picked me up, so I'd turn it on and for half an hour I'd just have to do my best. And I'd always make sure that however many high-fives, waves or handshakes I did on my way, Donna would be the last person I properly touched, or kissed, or had any interaction with before a game. She would be the last person I'd see before I went to work, did my job and did the best I possibly could, and the look she gave me before I went on would mean that somehow, in a millisecond, she focused me. There'd be a feeling of calm on the inside, even when on the outside I was being exuberant and jumping around.

In fact that exuberance was in its own way quite calming: sometimes I'd be more exuberant than I should have been, but I just had to burn off that nervous energy before a game. If I didn't, I'd be too tense and tight to get anything right. I'd want to explode.

I think it's worth considering what would happen if that did indeed happen. If I did actually explode. I've never seen it happen to someone in real life, but it might. You don't hear much about human combustion these days, do you? It's like quicksand – all the rage when I was a kid, when you couldn't move for people unexpectedly catching fire or meeting their demise in moist granular pits. But were it to happen to me I would, firstly, be very disappointed in myself that I couldn't control what I was doing. Then I'd be disappointed for people who'd come for a darts match and were now draped in bits of me, getting rather more than they'd bargained for with their chicken in the basket (a foot, a finger and so on). And then I'd feel sad for my family that they'd no longer have their son, uncle or confidant. That said, I do like to put on a show, and exploding into a thousand pieces would certainly be the ultimate show.

It's also worth thinking about how different darts players would respond to me literally exploding on stage. You can tell a lot about someone by how they respond to spontaneous human combustion. Were I to explode on stage I'd say Phil Taylor, for instance, would simply shrug and say it was only a matter of time – he was always telling me I needed to calm down. 'It's inevitable', he'd mutter, then go about his business. The likes of Kevin Painter, meanwhile, would think: 'Maybe I also need to wind it in a little, or it could happen to me.' Most of the others would just think: 'That's handy, I move up one space in the rankings.' (That's not too far-fetched – when you get a lot of darts players flying together on the same plane, the joke always comes that anyone not on the plane would be happy if it crashed. 'So-and-so would be thrilled, he'd move up to number one.')

As a commentator, I'm not sure how I'd react if I saw a human being go supernova. Some players would surprise me less than others: John Henderson is a gent of a man but he's a big lad, and there are some quite aggressive characters who need to calm it down a bit – I'd say Gary Anderson can get adequately irate, and could be a prime candidate for combustion.

Anyway. The pre-game practice boards are another place where rituals come into play. My own ritual on those boards was simple: my last three darts to the board would always be focused. I'd have to finish my practice routine off with three straight darts that hit 180, 140, or at least a ton. (It was once a 132 finish, but that became too difficult.) If I didn't get it, I'd try again. And again.

It became a little bit of a liability. The floor manager for Sky Sports or whichever channel I'd be on would give me two minutes, but I *needed* to hit those darts. If I didn't, I'd be in a frenzy. My nerves would be going as I tried to hit a decent score with the last three darts. Those last three practice darts would often see me being the most nervous I'd ever get at a darts championship – I could be all over the place and I wasn't even in front of the crowd yet. But somehow I'd always get what I needed in time. And once I'd got it, I was ready.

I wasn't the only one to feel the pressure on those practice boards. Some players made a big deal out of the fact that they'd only practise alongside certain other players. And then there's the players who, when there's a row of five practice boards, will only use their 'lucky' board. They think it brings them luck, though I'd question how lucky it is to end up brawling with another player because they've got your spot – I've seen arguments break out in a matter of seconds because one player or another supposedly wanted to be on a specific practice board.

In fairness, while I've never taken a swing at anyone for occupying 'my' board, I know where they're coming from when it comes to those practice sessions.

If you imagine a line of five practice boards, you'll find that everyone has their favourite spot. In my opinion, unless you're a bungling amateur, the first choice for all right-handers will be the one on the left; if that's gone, then your second choice should be the one on the right, and then obviously as a third choice you'll go for the one in the centre. If you're the fourth or fifth to arrive, you need to make a difficult choice but one thing's for sure, if you find yourself next to someone you're going to be distracted by what that other guy's doing. Sometimes that'll make you feel better about yourself, but at other times you'll walk away feeling a little inadequate. However much you might be pretending you haven't noticed, it's definitely not good for your confidence if you find yourself next to someone with a magnificent, powerful delivery – but for your own wellbeing you really need to be ignoring that magnificence. Obviously, if you happen to witness something pathetic, you'll offer a brief sideways look and a sad, supportive shake of the head in the moment, and you'll be damn sure you bring it up at a later date.

I must apologise for the previous paragraph. I started off writing about practice boards and somehow ended up talking about urinals.

7.

SPONSORSHIP

If the past is a foreign country, then for me the majority of the 1990s were North Korea: mostly decent weather but no internet. As the millennium approached, however, I got myself online and with my first email address came a very specific type of freedom: the freedom to send unsolicited emails to large corporations. Maybe I'd been influenced by too many viewings of *Field of Dreams*, but that film's optimistic 'if you build it, he will come' self-belief mantra was definitely on my mind when, having figured out how to send emails, I took it upon myself to find a sponsor. And I was thinking big.

'Hi,' I said in my emails to Adidas (!), TAG Heuer (!!) and Rolex (!!!). 'My name is Wayne Mardle and I'm a professional sportsman. I play darts, and I can guarantee your brand a minimum of 24 hours' live airtime when I play on television. I'd love to be associated with your brand. Do let me know if you require any further information.'

The 1990s may well have been a different time, but they weren't so different that Rolex, a luxury watch brand with nearly a century's experience in marketing its eye-wateringly expensive wristwear to royalty, billionaires and high-flyers based largely on principles of prestige and social cachet, were likely to throw money at a darts player nobody had ever really heard of. What can I say? I aimed high and I missed. I built it (sent an email) and he (the head of marketing at one of the planet's most luxurious lifestyle brands) most certainly did not come.

But do you know what did happen? Every single one of those brands I emailed – from Rolex to Adidas – got back to me. Not with the news I'd been hoping for, but with a kind response and best wishes for my career. So while those emails alone weren't exactly going to build me a swimming pool in my back garden, what they did give me was something that ultimately proved more valuable: a sense that if I persisted, I might one day get lucky. They gave me a sense of hope.

And as it happened soon after all this I did get lucky, albeit a little closer to home. My first ever sponsorship was through a mate, George Reeves. He was the boss of GL Reeves Engineering and a self-made man who, just as importantly, loved darts and also loved trying to help out players. My sponsorship fee? The princely sum of £3,000 – not big-league, perhaps, but enough to take some pressure off. So while I wasn't exactly arriving in pub carparks by private helicopter, what this cash injection did mean was that I could afford to do the Scottish Open, the Welsh Open, and a handful of European events.

The deal was simple: George gave me the three grand, then I'd give George 20 per cent of my winnings, and back then the chances of winning more than £15k in a year seemed remote to say the least, so I was happy. There was no contract; no 'sign this, sign that', just an honest businessman and a fledgeling darts player doing the best with what they had. We had mutual respect, and mutual trust as well. He never asked to see my books, I'd just send him his money in the post when I won some. Those were probably the only cheques I ever enjoyed writing.

Of course, with George sponsoring me that meant I'd be seen several times a year on TV, playing in the World Championship with GL Reeves Engineering emblazoned across my polo shirt. I'll discuss elsewhere how that simple garment eventually transmogrified into something a little more outlandish (and considerably more Hawaiian), but back then I couldn't have been happier keeping it simple in my GL Reeves top.

If you're interested in the intersection of sponsorship and darts shirt real estate economics, I'll begin with a story. A few years back I was hanging out in a Premier League practice room with One Dart himself, Peter Manley. Peter and I were chatting about what our shirts were worth sponsorship-wise. Peter was pointing at bits of his own shirt, going: 'This is seven grand, this is twelve, this is nine ...'

All in all his shirt was worth £35,000, and that was before he threw a single dart in the Premier League. Then we added mine up, and it came to £40,000. Forty grand, just to stand around on TV! Not to win. Not to do anything, really. Just to exist. Even when I lost every game, which I can assure you I more or less did, I was still paid £40,000 by companies who wanted promotion week in, week out: Falco Construction, CS Claringdon, Bet Direct, Harrows Darts. So I was sat there, thinking: 'I'm being paid way more than my old yearly wage, just for losing on TV. (I'm not a loser, I just lost a lot.)

Peter and I were feeling pretty pleased with ourselves at that point, and then Phil Taylor walked past. I asked him: 'Phil, you don't have to answer but how much is your shirt worth?'

He counted them one by one, and went: '£400,000.'

'Four hundred thousand,' I laughed, and I sat down before I fell down. And Phil just wandered off. The PDC have a limit of four sponsors per player, who can each have their logos on different parts of the shirt, and Phil was pulling in an average of more than twice my entire shirt's value, in every single one of his four spots. It's not that I felt intimidated, but it did kind of take the wind out of my sails. My £40,000 seemed a little less exciting now.

'There's no way he's ten times better than me,' I said to Peter.

Peter paused for a moment, thought about it, and replied: 'Actually, he probably is.'

When you're deconstructing the value of a darts shirt, one rule is not to make any assumptions about the players you'll see on TV. Some pros will be giving up spots on their tops for as little as £500 a pop, others for ten grand, and the likes of Michael van Gerwen will be in Phil Taylor-esque territory. But if you think a hundred grand seems pricey just to get your logo on a player's shirt, consider how many times that shirt will be seen by the millions of people who watch darts on TV.

In fact, this is something sponsors take into account. If you can say you're in the Premier League and that you'll be in seven other televised events during a year, that can prove to be quite a money spinner.

One of my smartest moves back in the day was when I let a potential sponsor know exactly how much airtime I'd had the previous year. In the space of twelve months I'd got to the final of the Desert Classic, the semi-final of the World Championship and the final of the World Matchplay. I said: 'I was on TV last year, in front of millions of viewers, for a total of 109 hours.' They couldn't believe it, but all the numbers added up, and even if you're charging Van Gerwen prices that's an obscene amount of airtime when you consider £100k would get you about two-and-a-half minutes' worth of ad break on, for instance, ITV. In fact if you look at the fact that airing a normal thirty-second ad can cost £20k, the 109 hours I quoted that sponsor represents about £4,360,000 of advertising time.

Doing the numbers now I do wonder if I undercharged them. (Snoop Dogg got a reported £5.3m for his Just Eat ad last year – I'd have done it for half that.) But my point is: sponsor a darts player and you're getting yourself a bargain. You'd think we could charge more, considering darts is now the second-biggest televised sport. But as things stand, getting your name on a darts player's shirt is one of the best value sponsorships anyone can be involved in.

Is that fair? That's out of my hands, sadly. The market rate is whatever people are prepared to pay, based on their own perception of value. If someone decides that the top prize in a *Call of Duty* world championship is worth hundreds of thousands of quid, or that the world's best drone flyer is worth throwing a million at, that's just the way it goes. Consider two four-bedroom houses, identical apart from the fact that one is in Hull and the other's in Mayfair. They're both big enough for the average family, but house prices in Hull are cheaper than they are in London, so the former costs £350,000 and the latter costs £3.5m. If you think of Mayfair as football and Hull as darts, you'll see why a champion in one sport gets ten times as much sponsorship cash. Mind you, I can tell you which neighbourhood I'd rather live in, and which sport I'd rather be involved with.

The best thing about sponsorships is that once you've got your first, you start your own journey from Hull to London as your perceived value increases, meaning that other sponsors decide to come knocking. It's quite something to see different brands trying to outbid each other – I always tried to do it as ethically as possible because nobody likes a piss-taker, but quite often they'd go backwards and forwards increasing the value of a sponsorship while I was caught in the middle wondering what was going on.

I never had a manager back then, so I'd be the one fielding all these calls and emails, but fortunately I had Donna around to knock sense into me if she felt I was making a bad decision, or getting into a tight spot. I would advise any player to have someone similar on their side, because darts players don't always make the smartest decisions when we're left to our own devices.

This is the warning to any player thinking they don't need a manager. Long story short, sponsors can give you cash up front in return for a percentage of your earnings. At one point early on I was at an event with another player and he explained that he had one sponsor who'd put up two grand and would take 50 per cent, plus a second sponsor who'd also put up two grand and would be taking ... 50 per cent. To you or me, it might seem obvious that he would be giving away 100 per cent of any winnings, but he had a different way of looking at it. He seemed to think that because the sponsors didn't know each other, there was a strong chance they'd each take the same 50 per cent. As far as he was concerned this was the heist of the century. A group of us spent the most frustrating half-hour of our lives attempting to talk sense into him, and to this day I still don't think he gets it. As it turned out he went out in the first round, won less than his sponsorship money, then pocketed the sponsors' £4k, so maybe this *was* the heist of the century, and maybe he was smarter than we gave him credit for.

(If he was not smarter than we gave him credit for, I dread to think how much he cost himself over the years.)

Quantity of sponsorship is one thing, but when it comes to the quality of sponsors you'll notice you don't tend to get Apple and Tesla – or Rolex – throwing money at players. Darts is a working-class game with working-class players and a largely working-class audience, so it makes sense that sponsors fit the demographic. Cigarette brand Embassy sponsored the BDO World Championship for decades. But there's definitely a reticence on the part of certain types of brand. I remember the first World Championship was sponsored by Skol beer, then Proton cars, but then it was Ladbrokes, and now it's William Hill. The second biggest event in the calendar is the Bet Victor World Matchplay.

With the gradual tightening of regulations around betting I do wonder how much longer betting companies will be permitted to dominate the sports world, and I believe the PDC need to put a lifeboat in the water just in case the current sponsorship falls away overnight. They should be lining up other sponsors who aren't in the betting industry. I know some companies don't want to be involved in darts because of how it was seen back in the day, but of course the longer certain sponsors are involved, the more it becomes a self-fulfilling prophecy. I really want someone like a Barclays Bank to come in to challenge the betting companies but, ironically, I don't fancy the odds of that happening any time soon.

Until that day comes, we can at least console ourselves with the fact that there's one product that'll always make sense bearing the face and name of a darts player. And that product is ... Well, it's literally a set of darts.

If you start doing well enough regularly enough there'll come a point when someone comes knocking, offering you the chance to have your own dart available. Everyone who plays has started off in a sports shop looking up at the racks of darts branded with big players' names, so as you'd expect it's a big rite of passage when you realise your own face will be on those racks alongside the greats.

Some sets come with rather strange sales pitches. I'm reminded of a certain player whose blushes I'll spare by referring to him here simply as 'Lohn Jowe'. He's never averse to making a buck, but you'll sometimes see something he's flogging and wonder if it's a mistimed April Fool's joke. A couple of years ago he had new darts come out, and upon unveiling them he said: 'These are the most aerodynamic darts ever. They get from A to B quicker than other darts. FACT.'

I can't have been the only one in the darts community to sense the distinct aroma of bullshit, but his spiel went on and on, and he was insistent in his claims. 'They've been tested, have they?' I asked. 'A robot repeatedly throwing these darts has been filmed in ultra-slow motion with each shot being timed in order to support your claims?'

'No,' he replied, 'I just tried them out and I think mine are quicker.'

You do have to respect the hustle. But that doesn't mean there isn't an extraordinarily fine line between hustle and outright nonsense.

As for my own darts, that moment of feeling like I'd finally arrived came in 2002. It was a simple proposition from a manufacturer: 'Wayne, we're going to make your darts for you, and we're going to give you £3,000.'

This sounded incredible, but I thought I'd chance my arm: 'Can I have some free sets of the darts as well?'

'Yes, we'll give you a hundred sets.'

This felt like a dream come true: I'd get some cash, a hundred sets to sell on, and most importantly I was going to see those darts on the shelf, with my face on, alongside all the big players. In my mind, I'd made it. When they first showed me the box I was totally in awe. 'Come knocking again next year,' they said, 'and we'll give you another three grand.' In that moment I felt like I'd become a darting superstar.

One day I got a call from the manufacturers with the good news that they were supplying one of the biggest equipment outlets in the country. Again, I won't name the outlet here but let's just say they're known for selling equipment related to sports directly to the consumer. The first thing I did was ask the exact date they'd be on sale. 'They're in there now,' came the reply. I was already winning events and playing World

Championships by this point, but the fact that I could now go into a shop and buy my own darts? That was an incredible feeling.

It was a feeling that didn't last as long as I might have hoped. Later that day I arrived at the Romford branch of Sports Direct. (The outlet was Sports Direct.) A new complex had just opened within Romford shopping centre – there was a cinema, a Sainsbury's and right in the corner a huge, gleaming, multi-floor Sports Direct with escalators everywhere. When I walked in that afternoon I felt the usual pull of the golf gear and while ordinarily I might have succumbed, this time I had somewhere else to be. I took the escalator to the first floor and eventually found what I was looking for. But it was not quite what I'd been expecting. The entire darts stand was about the width of an actual dartboard, and all I could see were Eric Bristow's darts and Dennis Priestley's darts. Their pictures and promotional cards were taking up almost the whole thing. Eventually Donna, who'd accompanied me, pointed out that right at the bottom of the display, in an ideal position to be kicked and dented by anyone who happened to be walking past, were exactly two sets of my own darts. I really can't express how big that branch of Sports Direct was, or how small the darts stand was, or how shoved at the bottom my darts were. It would be an understatement to say I was hugely disappointed.

I was tempted to rearrange them, reasoning that I should be a little bit higher, sitting alongside Eric and Dennis, but sometimes your family will give you the straight talk you need to hear, even when you don't want to hear it.

'Wayne,' Donna said, 'they're world champions. You're not.'

How we're still married in 2021 I have no idea. She's certainly a lucky lady. (If you see Donna please don't tell her I said this. Thank you in advance.) Either way, back there in that sports shop she put me right in my place. And my place, I'd learned, was basically on the floor. I'd made it, sure, but only a little bit. I'll never forget that dismal afternoon in Romford Sports Direct. There's probably a lesson there about not letting fame go to your head: I've seen some big mugs in Sports Direct over the years, but that day I felt like the biggest mug of all time.

I'd like to finish this chapter by saying that as it turned out I just needed to give it time. Over the years my darts rose up in the racks a little as my career took off, and what's more I didn't ever need to resort to any strange sales tactics regarding claims about aerodynamics.

But instead I'll finish this chapter with this inspirational, life-affirming message: Wayne Mardle darts are available now at hawaii501.com in a range of colours and weights, starting at just £40.

8.

SHOWMANSHIP

I don't generally feel comfortable bragging, but at the same time I'm writing a book that's using the whole darts angle as a thinly veiled excuse to talk about me and what I think about things, so concerns about ego went out of the window a long time ago and I'll just come out with it: there are only two true showmen in the world of darts. That's me and Bobby George. Fact.

Having idolised Bobby from a young age it was perhaps inevitable that my own darting composure wouldn't exactly be that of a man hiding from attention, but in all honesty I never really thought too much about the mechanics of putting on a performance until one day, instinctively, I simply started to do it. I'd always been confident in my ability on the dartboard, and there's always been a bit of swagger and cockiness when I've been playing, but when things started to pick up for me I found my personality took over. Once the ball started rolling, there was no stopping it: with his loud shirts and a louder mouth there was never any question over whether Wayne Mardle was in the house.

And as for those Hawaiian shirts ... Well, they deserve a whole book of their own. There was never a specific point when I thought: 'I'm going to do for darts what Madonna did for pop and become the darts world's very own queen of reinvention.' My personality didn't suddenly change overnight, but I do remember being at the BDO World Championship very early on and, as usual, all thirty-two participants were taking part in a parade before the first match. We'd be announced, we'd all walk on, everyone would clap and it would be a bit dull. And that particular year I noticed that nearly every single player wore black or blue. I remember thinking: 'For an exciting event, this is a very dull line-up of blokes.'

The only other colour in the line-up was a white shirt courtesy of Tony O'Shea, who stood out like a sore thumb, which in turn got me thinking about how I could, perhaps, also stand out a little. I wasn't exactly in love with my stage attire: in 2000 I'd played in the World Championship in a black t-shirt with The Mouth Of The South written on the back. I wanted rid of that name anyway, so I started to think about what I could do to shake things up.

This is the part in a movie where I'd be pulling a 'pondering' face – perhaps resting a finger on my chin and furrowing my brow – as the shot dissolved to the following year, when I found myself shopping in Vegas with my friend Dave Ansell and our wives, as you do. We were browsing in Premium Outlet (it's called fashion, look it up) and Dave disappeared for a minute, only to reappear from behind a pile of clothes brandishing a Hawaiian shirt. The garment was brilliantly grotesque: it looked like an acid trip in a paint factory. I'll never forget Dave's words: 'Look at THIS beauty.'

Well, despite the somewhat garish design I could see without a moment's hesitation that this was a piece of quality. It was clear to me, immediately, that the cut of a Hawaiian shirt would also mean it worked perfectly as a darts shirt. When I first laid eyes on that polyester marvel, priced at a hard-to-argue-with $4.99, it was love at first sight.

'I'm getting one of those for the Worlds,' I announced.

'No, you're not,' he said.

And of course within a minute I'd purchased one. So the genesis of my favourite shirt – a shirt I don't think it's hyperbole to describe as simply iconic – is really something that sounds more like the sort of excuse you'd expect to hear from a kid holding a football in front of a broken window: *it just kind of happened*. And of course once it was in my possession, there was no stopping me. In fact I started wearing that shirt so frequently that by the time that year's World Championship came around, I was already becoming known for it. All it had taken was one appearance on TV, and that was it. The crowd were wowed! Suddenly there were dozens of Hawaiian shirts in the crowd, and it grew from there.

I'd achieved my aim of standing out from the crowd. One thing's for sure, you're not going to blend into the background wearing a Hawaiian shirt, unless you literally happen to be in Hawaii, in which case you're actually wearing camo gear and may be mistaken for a deserter from the Hawaiian army: not to be advised.

They say that with great power comes great responsibility and the same is true of outlandish garments, except in my case instead of power it's Hawaiian shirts, and instead of responsibility it's lots of other people wearing Hawaiian shirts. In 2003, not long after I'd unveiled my shirt, I was with my mum, dad and Donna in Blackpool and we went to the shops to waste an afternoon.

We found ourselves in a Primark-esque clothing establishment where I got bothered a bit for autographs, and back then fame was new to me so I was having great fun spending time with the small crowd that was gathering around me. After those people had dissipated, the proprietor of the shop, who'd realised who I was, came over. He seemed very pleased to meet me, and shook me firmly by the hand.

I said: 'What's that for?'

He went: 'I've had Hawaiian shirts in stock for years, and thanks to you I've finally got rid of the lot.'

That started a thought process. Here, in the Hollywood version of this book (and please do send all offers to me c/o the publisher), there would be another dissolve, this time from that slightly over-enthusiastic handshake in Blackpool to the busy workshop of a gentleman in east London. That's where, at the end of 2004, with the help of an investment from a man by the name of Ron, six thousand Mardle-inspired Hawaiian shirts were being knocked up.

I got those shirts made for a fiver each and sold them for £25 a pop – they sold out (eventually) and to this day I still see them at darts events. Resilience is just one of the many benefits of polyester. Those things are indestructible. Not so good for the environment, I'm afraid – and in ten millennia I wouldn't be surprised if six thousand Hawaiian shirts are all that's left of human civilisation – but great if you're not keen on ironing. It transpired that you could leave them in their original packaging for the best part of half a decade and they'd come out completely creaseless.

More importantly, being basically plastic, they're disconcertingly water resistant. I've fallen up steps and spilt booze on myself too many times to mention; I've had entire pints dropped over me by over-enthusiastic darts fans. I've had someone in the audience hawk up a big ball of phlegm and spit it in my direction. My pride? Dented on each of those occasions. My shirt? No signs of any booze or bodily fluids at all. When you're wearing polyester any liquid just bounces right off. I remember once, after a full pint landed on me on my way to the stage, one of the officials said to me: 'Do you want to wait a minute so you can get changed?' I just wiped myself down and got on with it.

Once I'd established my Hawaiian shirt image, it wasn't long before I'd got myself new walk-on music – it could only have been the theme from late sixties US cop show *Hawaii Five-O*. All I can really say about the *Hawaii Five-O* theme, and you'll be aware of this if you ever saw any of my walk-ons, is that it's absolutely impossible not to run around to. Fire up YouTube now and whack it on, you'll be aeroplaning round your house within twenty seconds. I may be biased here but I do think that song is one of the greatest instrumental TV bangers of all time, somewhere between the *Blockbusters* theme and the music off *Ski Sunday*.

(Sidenote: TV shows used to have such brilliant music, didn't they? The best you can hope for these days on a Netflix drama is two seconds of a whooshing noise over a black screen with the title written in a white sans-serif font. Bring back proper TV theme tunes. Or just put the *Ski Sunday* music on everything.)

If you want to be a showman in the world of darts, you need to get your walk-on right, and music's just one part of that. Darts takes skill and practice but walking onto the stage is a skill in its own right, and if you want to learn how to get it spot on, look to the masters. I get goosebumps when Michael van Gerwen's due on and the room goes dark, the walk-on music starts, and the green lasers fire up.

In fact I'm getting goosebumps just thinking about it now. That's what a perfect walk-on's all about: the game's not even started yet, they won't even blow the whistle for another ten minutes, and you're already mesmerised by what's in front of you and excited about what's about to happen. Michael's walk-on music is inspired, too – he was using The White Stripes' 'Seven Nation Army' long before it was retitled 'Oh, Jeremy Corbyn' by a load of students in 2017. Anyway, to me it will always be 'Oh, Michael van Gerwen'.

Having mentioned the sublime I must now consider the ridiculous, and I have to say, largely because it never happened to me, the funniest thing that can ever happen with a walk-on is when the entire room's poised for a dramatic entrance, the whole place is ready to go berserk, the player's feeling the first rush of adrenaline and ... the wrong music starts up. Imagine anyone other than me having to walk on to the *Hawaii Five-O* music! Chaos ensues; people go berserk. What happens next? Are they going to stop the music? Are you going to have to walk out anyway? Nobody has a clue apart from the person who's in charge of the music and he's probably nipped out for a fag as soon as he's hit play. And what you don't always see on TV is the floor manager shouting and waving their arms around – 'STAY THERE!!!' 'GO!' 'NO, STAY THERE!!' – while the proper music's being sorted out or, sometimes, not.

In considering ridiculousness I also find my mind wandering back in the direction of John Part. His nickname Darth Maple I have covered already, but it bears repeating that Darth Maple simply doesn't work because 'maple' doesn't sound like 'Vader' and 'Darth' doesn't actually mean anything. When it came to Part's walk-on, however, the *Star Wars* motif was beaten to within an inch of its life. His entrance was soundtracked by the 'Imperial March' and, depending on how much spare change John had rattling around in his pocket that day, involved anything from John waving around a knock-off light sabre that looked like he'd picked it up in a hurry from the nearest Argos, to the sight of John flanked by Poundland stormtroopers, a threadbare Wookie or someone who'd apparently been given five minutes' notice that they were expected to dress up as Princess Leia.

John and I are friends today, and off the board we were friends before. On it we were enemies, and it's often said I was one of his fiercest competitors, but he's a three-time world champ and I'm, well, not, so that's that. Could it be sour grapes prompting me to claim his walk-on is useless, didn't work, doesn't work and never will work? That's not for me to say.

But the point is he sticks by it, despite repeated and dare I say slightly heroic attempts by myself and others to convince him that his walk-on music should instead be '(You Gotta) Fight for Your Right (To Party!)' by The Beastie Boys. The song's (a little) heavy on the parentheses (for my liking!) but we all call him Party and it would be perfect.

His response, whenever any of us brings it up? 'Don't like it.'

'John! It's not about you. This is about the experience! Getting the crowd on your side. You can't be doing this with *Star Wars*! It's just wrong!'

'Don't care.'

We keep trying; he refuses to buckle. I appreciate a man who stands his ground but this is extremely poor behaviour from the three-time world champ. John is annoyingly stubborn.

Which isn't to say there weren't times when I might have had second thoughts about that monster I'd created for my own walk-ons: the Wayne Mardle who always gave it the full-on 'circus coming to town' treatment whenever the camera was on him. If I'm honest there can come a point where you end up feeling slightly trapped in a set of expectations, or haunted by the thought: *I need to make the entertainment*. And so thoughts do turn to those players who haven't been surrounded by razzmatazz. If you think back to Eric Bristow, for example, he didn't rely on any of that kind of showmanship. He simply had, within him, the swagger and the confidence that said: 'I'm comfortable as I am.' The thousands of eyes on every throw? Not a problem. The TV cameras? Not a problem. I'm not saying he didn't relish the attention, but he didn't go out of his way to court it either.

Looking back on the days when I'd run around in ludicrous shirts, there was never a point when I felt, 'I *have* to do this', but I do have a strong sense that maybe I wanted to be liked, and maybe I wanted to be different, but I think what I really wanted was to be remembered. It definitely took away some of the anxiety of being on stage, and gave me a way to get rid of the nervous energy that could have distracted me from playing well. It's also true that being a showman, and being that much of an entertainer, was to the detriment of my game from time to time.

But putting on a performance was part of my thing, and I wouldn't change it for the world. The more you give the crowd, the more they then give *you* when you need it. There can be a big moment coming up in your game and you're not thinking about yourself. Instead you're thinking: 'Get it – they'll go mad'. I never got into darts to perform – I just liked the look of the dartboard. But I ended up being a performer, and performers like to be liked. I've said this many times over the decades but I'll say it again now in print: if there's someone in that audience who's watching two players and they don't know which one to support, I'll go out of my way to make sure they end up supporting me.

9.

HOBBY VS SPORT

Historically there's been fraught debate over whether darts is just a hobby or qualifies as a sport, and that's often hinged on precisely how people define 'sport' itself. There's the element of physical competition, of course, but by that definition sports should include Hungry Hippos and queuing to get on your flight when you book with a budget airline. Another thought is that it's all down to being able to do something to a high level of technical ability, but again, I had a plumber round last week who did a great job of cleaning out my drains and I don't think either she or I would suggest that Sky Sports should start showing formation cistern-fitting.

Someone might also be regarded as a sportsperson if they've achieved a certain level of fitness. This is where darts may have fallen down in the past, and it's often claimed that darts shouldn't be a sport simply because the people who play it are not always, shall we say, at the very peak of physical prowess.

On the other hand, if darts is going to be judged on the basis of athleticism then by that logic all athletes should therefore be good at darts, but don't tell me just because Cristiano

Ronaldo is one of the fittest men on the planet he could play darts better than me, because he couldn't and I hereby challenge him to a darts match any time he likes. Just because darts players aren't stereotypical athletes, that doesn't mean we're not sportspeople.

A more constructive view of the debate is that sport hinges on people being able to do their competitive thing, day in, day out, time and time again, to a level that makes them professional. Make no mistake: darts really is a difficult, technical sport, and until you've tried it over a sustained period you won't know how physical it actually is. To a doubter, I'd say this: stand in front of a board, throw for thirty minutes, make your last throws as accurate as your first, and by the way tell me how your arm's feeling afterwards. As for how your arm and entire upper torso were feeling the next morning ... Well, I'd recommend stocking up on Deep Heat.

In any case the sport-versus-not-actually-a-sport debate came to an end on 24 March 2005, when Sport England finally announced that, yes, they would accept darts as a sport. 'This,' the BDO's Olly Croft said at the time, 'is one of the greatest days in the history of darts.'

If I'm honest, if you ignore the tax implications which I won't detail here because you and I each have finite time on this planet and the less of that spent discussing tax the better, almost nothing changed on a day-to-day basis when darts become a sport. I didn't need a box being ticked on a bit of official paper to regard darts as a sport – to me it always had been. It's not like on 23 March 2005 we were toiling away, throwing darts by candlelight in dilapidated Dickensian hovels, and at the stroke of midnight the life of a darts player became a never-ending jamboree of bountiful feasts, palm trees and conga lines. The shift meant a lot to dart manufacturers and people trying to 'sell' darts, but to your average player pretty much the only noticeable change was the immediate introduction of random drug tests.

The issue of drugs in darts is a strange one. I always found it hard to imagine what sort of drugs you could take to make yourself any better. You're not going to have much chance of a treble 20 when you're off your trolley on ketamine, and you don't want to be tripping on acid when John Part's wandering around with some some bloke dressed as a Wookie. I've discussed this with a lot of people when drug tests have come up – although as I'll discuss elsewhere in this book, there are plenty of those players who'll insist their game is made better by alcohol, a substance that outside darts doesn't generally help you get better at *anything* other than shouting and walking into things. But in darts it's viewed as something that can relax you, make you lose your inhibitions and reduce anxiety, and on reflection I expect people feel the same way about cocaine and marijuana, the two most common drugs to turn up in testing in sport.

I got tested myself, actually, just after losing yet another world semi-final, this time against Kirk Shepherd in 2008. This was the fifth time I'd gone out in the semis. It was a strange time to decide I needed testing: I was clearly inconsolable because I'd just endured the latest in a long line of depressing semi-final performances, so let's just say I didn't look like a man who'd taken anything performance enhancing – and I definitely hadn't played like one.

One of the more questionable bannings happened to Richie Burnett, a former world champion, who tested positive after an event. His explanation for the entire sorry situation was that someone had put marijuana in cakes he'd eaten, and that he didn't know. I expect your bullshitometer might be on the verge of exploding here, so maybe I should tell you a thing or two about Richie because the more you know about him, the more you'll understand how he's precisely the sort of person to whom improbable and stupid things happen.

For instance, back in 1995 when he was skint and due to appear in a tournament, he had a cost-saving brainwave: he'd travel from Wales to the tournament with a suitcase full of Pot Noodles. All he'd need was hot water from a kettle. Now, the problem was that not all hotel rooms have tea- and coffee-making facilities, so Richie had to make a quick decision. That decision, he later told me, was to bleed a radiator into his Pot Noodle. Darting genius though he is, that's pretty much the level of Richie Burnett's thought process, and hopefully this illustrates how plausible it is that he might, indeed, have accidentally eaten one or two hashcakes.

In any case drug tests are an inevitable part of darts being considered a Proper Sport. And there's a line of thought that says if we must accept the rough, perhaps we could also get a bit of smooth. If darts really is considered proper, shouldn't it therefore be eligible for the Olympics?

On paper there's no reason it shouldn't. There are already loads of Olympic sports that rely on getting one thing near or into another thing. Is curling any more or less worthy than darts? Is archery really any different, apart from the fact that a bow and arrow is bigger, requires more materials during manufacture and more space on aircraft when being transported, and is therefore worse for the environment? You could suggest darts requires less physical movement than either of those, but then how do you explain shooting, a ludicrous so-called sport in which a rifle does all the hard work and the greatest physical exertion is the competitor moving their trigger finger?

The other question would be whether darts would count as a summer sport or a winter one, and the answer you give here is important because it could make the difference between the great and the good of the darts world hanging out with either sprinters (serious, reliable) or luge enthusiasts (obvious imbeciles).

My instinct here, given darts' traditional indoor vibes combined with the crackle of a roaring pub fire being baked into the sport's DNA, is that it should be part of the winter Olympics. To that end I'd also suggest that if there's no problem building a ramp for ski jumping and an ice rink for skating, the Olympic committee should invest serious cash in constructing meticulous recreations of authentic British boozers in which the world's greatest darts players can compete. Jukebox blaring out assorted Queen B-sides, toilet roll shoved down the basins for no discernible reason, sudden punch-up in the carpark outside: the works.

Despite my flight of fancy, darts never will be in the Olympics. At least not if I have anything to do with it. I don't expect I'm ever likely to be called up by the Olympic committee with a view to rethinking the whole thing from the ground up, but if they do ever make this hypothetical phonecall I expect it will be with the intention of sounding me out on the potential inclusion of darts, and if so I may well shock them. My belief is that for an Olympic medal to mean anything, winning it needs to represent the pinnacle of any particular sport. For the 100-metre sprint, for instance, being an Olympic gold medallist is something every sportsperson trains for and dreams of. If you're a fan of running in a straight line but not for very long, there's no better medal you can win. But ask yourself this: when was the last time you heard anyone described as an Olympic footballer? When it comes to darts I'd still rather win the World Championship, World Matchplay or the Premier League over being an Olympic champion. If I were offered an Olympic gold medal I'd be more than happy to accept it, but only because I know I'd definitely be able to shift it on eBay.

So my proposal to the Olympic bigwigs would be simple and, dare I say it, rather heroic: rather than *adding* things like darts, the best way of moving forward would be to simply remove a load of other stuff. Two weeks is too long anyway, I'm sure they could get the whole thing done in nine days. I want track, I want field, I'm prepared to accept a combination of the two, but pretty much everything else should be binned off.

It's bad news for artistic swimming. It's even worse news for anything involving horses. And for the avoidance of doubt and with apologies to Tom Daley and pals my proposed cull does therefore include diving, which in my book is simply glamorous falling. I want to see people outside and I want to see them running around and jumping over things; nearly everything else can be consigned to the Olympic dustbin alongside other former Olympic sports like *jeu de paume* (?), offshore power-boat racing (!) and tug of war (?!?).

Although darts' recognition as a sport has legitimised it to outsiders, and I wouldn't swap my former career as a professional for anything, in my book it's fine for new players to see darts simply as a hobby or as a recreational pleasure.

Something I see a lot now, which was never the case when I was starting out, is people getting into darts at an extremely young age. I may have got into it when I was very young but I was the exception, and I was often surrounded by people twice my age. And the reason kids are starting out younger, I think, is that darts players have become more visible on the TV, meaning that more than ever before there's a clear route to being able to make a living out of life on the oche. 'Mummy, I want to be a darts player' – you'd never have heard that thirty or forty years ago, but these days it's most definitely A Thing.

There's the financial aspect, too. In the last five years the money flying around in the game has increased to the point where people are drifting towards darts simply as a way of making money. The way parents see kids playing darts now is how parents saw their kids playing football in the eighties. The whole scene of getting excited on Sunday mornings because 'there's a scout turning up!' or 'my kid's going to be a footballer'? That's now happening in darts. The kids might just be throwing for fun but it's the parents with pound signs in their eyes: they've seen that there are numerous players who can earn over a million quid a year, and that below that it's quite possible to earn between £200k and £700k, even without being a champion.

And when I say people are getting into it young, I mean *really* young. I get sent videos all the time – 'Wayne, help my son or daughter out with their throw' – then I'll watch the video and it's of a four-year-old. Putting to one side the rather alarming safety angle, I always go back with one piece of advice: 'Let them enjoy it, and just see where it takes them. If they're still playing in a couple of years, let's talk again.' It's also worth remembering that darts, unlike something like football or gymnastics, doesn't need to be a young person's sport. So many great players, from John Lowe to Bobby George, picked up their first dart in their mid-twenties and thirties. There's no rush!

The key part of that advice I give those parents? *Let them enjoy it.* I didn't take up darts because I wanted to be a professional. Ask any professional darts player and they'll tell you the same thing: we started out because we loved it. Passion might only get you so far down the road, but you'll never get anywhere without it.

The other problem with going straight from your bedroom to qualifying school to becoming a professional, almost overnight, is that you're losing the learning curve that's made so many darting greats as great as they are.

And part of that learning curve is losing. You've got to be able to handle a disastrous situation, and the next time you play you've got to be able to pull yourself together. You need to go through that cycle again, and again, and again. I've heard it so many times, even from people like Phil Taylor: 'It was really hard tonight,' they'll say after losing, 'I didn't feel comfortable at all.' And yet, the next weekend, they've taken part in another event and they've won. That sort of resilience is vital in being a darts professional, but you don't get that resilience without having been a darts amateur first.

When people go straight from their bedroom to the glare of TV cameras the entire 'player in the pub' part of most former champions' careers is taken out of the equation. But it's in that pub, club and exhibition setting that you learn so much about gameplay: your own, and other people's. I think of all the endless league games in pubs and tournaments I did in my own teens, on the road to eventually becoming a professional, and I see them as my apprenticeship. Where would The Beatles have been if they'd never played the Cavern Club, or slogged their way through forty-eight nights in Hamburg for £2.50 a night?

The point is, one does not simply decide to be a darts professional. A few years back a fella called Justin Irwin wrote a book called, and I take my hat off to him here, *Murder on the Darts Board*. The idea for the book was this: in January 2005, he abruptly resigned from his well-paid job, and threw everything he had into just one goal: going from being a nobody, to qualifying for the World Darts Championship in one year. He posted online and I spoke to him as a result. The gist of the conversation was: 'I'm going to pack in my job and become a professional darts player – how hard can it be?'

At the time I thought: 'How dare he think it's that simple?' I thought he was a twat to start with, but he's a good lad. As we got to know each other better I realised he was actually setting out to prove how hard it was, not how easy it was. (Me? Misunderstanding something? Never.) And yes, he got better after hours of practice, but by the end of the whole thing he was so far off being good enough that he realised what a ridiculous idea it had all been. Even if he'd given himself *ten* years, it's unlikely he would have made it.

Practising alone won't always get you there. I think about some of the guys I played alongside when I was thirteen; they've practised for thirty-five years, they're still playing now and, bless them, they're as bad today as they were back then. They've not got better through practice. Or through watching others and learning. That's because darts is – newsflash – actually quite difficult. If you want to smash it, you actually need talent.

You'll hear a lot of people talk about the ten thousand hours idea, popularised by writers like Malcolm Gladwell and Matthew Syed, who reckoned that you could become an expert in anything if you put in the required number of hours.

Fascinating insight there but the thing is, anyone who does *anything* for ten thousand hours is going to get better at it – but will they ever be good enough?

Think of it this way: all darts professionals might well have put ten thousand hours into their game, but that doesn't mean everyone who puts in that many hours is going to become a professional. To put it another way, I could go in for ten thousand hours' vocal training but I'll never be the next Adele. And I really mean that. Because I talk loudly people often think I can sing, and for a while I believed it myself – the result of which is that I went through a period, rather longer than it should have been, when I thought I sounded like Macy Gray. A sort of tuneful Marge Simpson. I really did a job on myself. I was convinced I could sing, when in fact I couldn't carry a tune in a bucket. Macy Gray had this song, 'I Try', and I thought I sounded so much like her that I sang 'I Try' after being introduced on stage in front of six thousand people at the O2 in Leeds. I was having a great time. The crowd were not. Their response was, shall we say, not as enthusiastic as I might have hoped. Which is to say: they laughed. Someone showed me the recording afterwards and I thought: 'Hm, I won't be doing that again.'

The mistake I'd made was in thinking that just because I enjoyed doing something, I was actually any good at it. So these days I keep it simple: I play darts on stage, and I sing in the shower, and never the twain shall meet. And you know what? I love belting out songs when I'm on my own, just as thousands of amateur sportspeople enjoy throwing, kicking, running and jumping.

Over on Hackney Marshes, not too far from where I grew up as a kid, there are twenty-five football pitches all backed onto each other, and each weekend you can go down there and see dozens of men and women nursing hangovers as they try to kick a ball about to the best of their ability. They'll be competitive, but at the end of the day – when they're usually back in the pub – they've just been having a bit of fun with their mates. That's what it's all about.

When I think about being sixteen years old, I remember travelling round with Donna from one holiday camp to another with other players. We were all part of a little family – admittedly, a family that was playing to try and nick money out of each other's pockets, but a family all the same. You'd play someone, you'd beat them, they'd buy you a drink, you'd go for a Chinese and get pissed together. That's where friendships were made.

What sticks with me most isn't who won what or who lost to whom, it's the camaraderie, the fun and the memories that were created. For all the talk about darts being a professional concern, and how it's now a sport with big endorsements and even bigger prizes, darts should always begin as a hobby and a passion. And for most players, that's all it ever needs to be.

10.

MONEY

In 2002 I earned my first pound as a darting professional. I'd been booked to take part in an event at a pub called the Damory Oak at Blandford Forum in Dorset. By this point I was already a world semi-finalist and playing for England, and had won big ranking events, but this otherwise unremarkable event was special: I'd given up my job at the Association of Accounting Technicians on the Friday, and on the Saturday I was off to Dorset for my first exhibition as a fully-fledged professional.

I'll never forget the feeling of excitement as Donna and I drove up there: it was as if I'd been given a new lease of life. 'This,' I told myself, 'is my *job*.' It was a great night and I took home £400 – the equivalent of a week's pay at the job I'd just packed in.

In the years that followed I stayed in the top echelon for over a decade, experienced many highs and many more lows, and won some good money along the way. None of which was anything I'd been accustomed to growing up.

Even that first £400 payout was a far cry from the sort of money I grew up around – my mum was a machinist and my dad worked for the Post Office, so mine was a solid working-class childhood, with food on the table and the kids looked after, but not a huge amount of extra cash flying around for luxuries.

That said, there were opportunities to top up the kitty. My Uncle Peter and Auntie Sylvia ran an antiques shop down Portobello Road and they'd often do house clearances, on the hunt for treasure that'd been left behind by previous residents with less of an eye for an item's true value. Very often they'd come across an item potentially worth a huge amount, and they'd find that they could spruce it up and offload it to the posh west London crowd with a hefty mark-up. But the trash they couldn't get rid of (or wasn't likely to attract much attention from the more hoity-toity end of their client base) ended up in the back of my dad's big blue Luton van.

Much like my later career in darts, what started off as a hobby for my dad quickly proved to be a decent income stream. In my early teens I started doing boot fairs with my family – Hackney Wick car boot, where the greyhound stadium used to be, was a regular spot. Most Sundays we'd find ourselves unpacking at 6am, and if you've ever done a boot fair yourself you'll know all about the early-morning lurkers who pretty much rip old tat out of your hands before you've even finished unloading the rest of the items. I couldn't believe the prices people were paying: there were atrocious-looking vases sold for £300, wonky church organs for £400 ... 'How much is it? I'll take it now!'

As time went by I got my own little piece of the stall, and that really brought me out of my shell. I was thirteen by this point – my dad would price up all the items and say: 'Don't ever take less than what's on that ticket.' But I soon figured out that if someone was trying to haggle me down from a fiver I could make a counter-offer, suggesting that for £6 I'd throw in another item. They didn't need to know that the second item had been knocking around for ages and didn't have a chance in hell of selling; they thought they were getting a bargain, and my addition of a worthless trinket had added an extra quid to our day's take. 'Make the customer happy, Wayne' – sage advice from wise parents.

I have to admit I didn't always enjoy those early mornings back then. You want to be doing your own thing at that age, and getting up at 4am on a Sunday is rarely any teenager's definition of Your Own Thing. My sister, who was twenty-one by then, had her own life and wanted no part of our car-boot shenanigans, meaning it was usually just me and my parents.

Despite the early mornings, looking back on the time I got to spend with my mum and dad I really appreciate what a special period it was. We'd get a Kentucky takeaway on the way home, because everyone was so tired, and then as a family we'd count the takings. We had those pouches that tie round your waist, like a milkman would have had, and my dad would empty them out onto the dining table. Some days there'd be the better part of a grand. He'd fish out a note and say: 'There's your twenty.'

Twenty quid for a twelve-hour day may not seem like much, but (a) this was the eighties, when £20 would get you a deposit on a two-bed flat just outside the M25, and (b) I was thirteen, and all money was good money.

I've always worked for my money but little did I know, when I was taking that twenty quid from the kitchen table, that a few years later I'd be able to take charge £15,000 for two hours' work. Not to be sneezed at, although when you do the numbers you'll see that the length of your average one-second sneeze would still make you £2.

I hasten to add that big paydays like that didn't come along every day, but one such moment did occur when I was booked to take part in a pro–celebrity pairs event in Germany about five years ago. I was flown in and flown out, I played with a German sports presenter called Laura Wontorra, I didn't even have to win, and they wired me the cash the next day. It was an incredible payday for what was essentially an exhibition, and to top the lot I got a selfie with football legend Lothar Matthäus while I was there, which was probably worth £15k in its own right.

However much you might get paid on the occasional good day, everything seems to even out when you take into account the occasional extremely bad day. One bad day came for me many years ago, when I took part in a tournament that turned out not to be everything it promised to be. I was playing alongside some pretty big names and back then I'd generally be taking home between £3,000 and £10,000 for that kind of event, so the promised £15,000 seemed almost too good to be true.

Reader, it was indeed too good to be true. We were beginning to sense something fishy might be going on when we asked, early on in the week, when they'd be needing our bank details. 'Give them to us later on,' we were all told. 'There's no rush.' At the end of the week the full horror of the situation became clear: none of the players got paid. The organisers of the event knocked us. I'll never know whether it was an unforeseen fiasco or a con from the start, but the event was packed all week, so I can't imagine it was anything to do with ticket sales. Maybe the £15k I went on to earn at that German pro–celebrity match was the universe's way of saying sorry.

Whether it was cosmic rebalancing or coincidence (spoiler: it was coincidence), that only needs to happen once before you become a little bit smarter about payments. If you win through the PDC they already have your details and you'll get your cash in your account a week or two later, but I've had all sorts of payments over the years: bank transfer, cheque, sacks stuffed with unmarked banknotes …

Well, I presume they were unmarked. I've no reason to assume any organisations I've done business with are suspected of being involved in money laundering and there's no cause for the authorities to be interested in how I much I spend at Asda. The main reason for specifying they were unmarked is that after years of watching heist movies I consider a bag of unmarked banknotes to sound incredibly exciting, and when you get to my age you look for thrills where you can get them.

As for the fact that I've been paid in cash, well, I've done some corporate events in eastern European countries where I've been paid in dollars and it's been heavily suggested I squirrel the cash away under my bed rather than declare it to the taxman. (Or taxwoman for that matter – it's 2021, after all, and I believe it's important we view the ability to send scary letters and be generally avoided in social situations as a lifestyle choice that's open to all.)

I've had similar offers in the UK, too. 'Wayne,' they'll say, 'will you come and do an exhibition at our working men's club?'

'I'd love to! I charge £1,500.'

There's a pause on the other end of the line and I know exactly what's coming: 'How much would you charge for cash?'

'Let me have a think,' I say. I pause dramatically, allowing the caller to imagine me recalculating my fee. And then I say: 'Okay, how about £1,500?'

They don't get it. The point is, whether they pay me by cash, cheque, bank transfer, bitcoin or in a complex bartering system involving lifestock and bags of grain I'm putting it all through legitimately, so it's the same price. It's childish, I know, but I do relish that pause before giving them precisely the same fee.

The mistake I think they generally make is to assume just because I look like a window cleaner I'll accept payment on the same terms. No, thank you. How they want to cook their books is up to them, but while they might be doing themselves a favour they're certainly not doing me one.

Maybe it's my belief that tax avoidance is best left to comedians and members of Take That; maybe it's my belief that it's important the more well-off among us put something back into the pot for those less fortunate; maybe it's the fact that I don't want to go to prison, and maybe it's a combination of all three, but I declare every penny I earn: I put down my expenses, I put down my fee, and the whole thing's totally above board. I've been randomly investigated twice in my career and that whole sorry farrago is stressful enough when everything *is* in order. I want to make sure that if I'm ever investigated again everything's beyond clean.

Another thing from the You Have Got To Be Having A Laugh file is when organisers try it on based on what's already in my calendar. 'I see you're in Pontefract in two weeks,' they'll say. 'We're in Leeds, which is only half an hour away – would you do us half price the night after?' The 'while you're down there' line of enquiry usually shuts down shortly after I ask why I don't reduce my fee for Pontefract and charge Leeds full price. It's unfair on one venue if I give others a discount just because I happen to be in the area – particularly when the first venue is the reason I'm in that area in the first place!

'Would you still like to book me?' I ask.

'Yes please, Wayne,' they say. Then it's happy days.

I started this chapter by mentioning the first money I ever earned as a professional darts player, but just as significant for me was the last few quid I took as a pro. It was 11 June 2011, and I earned £200 for a win over Dave Ladley, before going on to lose the next game to Co Stompé, 6–4. That was that. I didn't win another penny in my professional darts career.

And the reason I bring that up is that at the time I had no idea that would be my last £200. Nor does any player when they inevitably find themselves in the same situation. You know that thing they say about growing up as a kid, and how one day you'll find yourself out riding your bike with your best mates for the very last time, it's just that nobody realises? It's the same when you're chucking tungsten at some sisal. As the dart leaves your hand, you have no idea it'll be the last professional dart that makes you any money.

That's a realisation that comes in the hours, days and months that follow. Sometimes it takes years to realise you're a spent force, and that's a problem if you're still haemorrhaging cash. Unfortunately we see money mismanagement left, right and centre in darts, to the point where I feel the Professional Dart Players Association should have an obligation to make sure players are looking after their money.

There are a few reasons players get into tricky situations, and one of them is that we're generally working-class human beings – we're not normally from university-educated backgrounds, and we haven't usually grown up with loads of cash around. With all that can come the 'pub' mentality: easy come, easy go. If you've just won a large sum of money, whether that's twenty grand or ten times that, it's easy to find yourself in a mindset where you just assume forklift trucks laden with riches will continue whirring up your driveway forever.

And it's hard, when you suddenly receive a nice chunk of cash, to stay focused on the empty months on the horizon. There are big paydays in darts, but those are days with very little in between. You'll go for months with nothing, then you'll earn £40k, then there are months of nothing again. You've got to look after it while you're bringing it in. Top tip: don't blow the lot on a Mercedes if you're still living with your mum.

There are old players today who've reached a stage in life when they should be making the most of their free bus pass or putting their feet up in front of *The Chase*, but who are still having to tout themselves out on the exhibition circuit. All because they over-extended in the years when they were making money, didn't realise they were on the slide until it was too late, and will have to spend the rest of their lives making up for it. The scary thing is, there are players on the circuit right now who are pulling in near to £300k a year and spending the whole lot on absolute nonsense, not realising there'll come a point next year, the year after that or the year after *that* when their £300k a year has slumped to £50k a year. That slide will only continue.

Add in the complication of an unexpectedly severe tax bill and you can be left with nothing. It's really easy to fall into the trap of thinking when someone earns a million they actually *get* a million – but when it's your own money, you need to know what's yours and what's going to HMRC. Even when I was back doing a day job I understood that the figure at the bottom of my payslip was rather a lot less than the figure at the top. Adrian Lewis is an example of someone who's been caught out here – he earned a lot of money in a short space of time but he famously said after winning the world title and £200,000: 'This is basically all going to the taxman.' That's doing it wrong.

Facing the void at the end of a career? It's happened before, it will happen again. And I'm aware of how easily it could have happened to me. Going back to the age of thirty-eight, I was finished as a darts player. I think of that a lot. I was lucky that I could go into commentary and was – and still am – sought after on the exhibition and corporate scene, but not every player can do that, and some go from a professional player to nothing at all. So to anyone who's earning a lot of money right now, I ask: could you carry on your lifestyle even if you'll be earning less money next year, then even less the year after that? If the answer is yes, you're fine. If the answer is no, get your accountant on the phone right now.

In any case, frugality is nothing to be scared of. I rather admire those players who've absolutely coined it in but go about their lives with no outward display of wealth. Terry Jenkins, who's been out of professional darts for a while but was a prolific and successful player in his time, made a tidy sum on the oche but you'd never have guessed it by looking at him or the car he drives. The last time I saw him he was pootling about in a battered Kia Sedona whose resale value I'd estimate as being somewhere in the region of a decent condition three-seater Chesterfield sofa and a late-nineteenth-century walnut dining table – and in the back of it was a well-used commode.

In fairness Terry was dabbling in antiques at that point, one man's second-hand poochair is another man's priceless heirloom, and at the end of the day you only need to get caught short once in traffic to put in place alternative arrangements; but you'd hardly look at Terry going about his business and guess he was sitting on a tidy sum. I think Terry's squirrelled it all away. What for? Who knows!

Even players who lead rather opulent lives can be surprisingly careful with their money. Michael van Gerwen undoubtedly likes to lead an extravagant existence, disappearing off to the Maldives on holiday and living life in the fast lane, but at the same time he's quite brilliantly put most of his wealth into buying his house, a sprawling bespoke home that's unlikely to lose its value. He's sitting on a pile. 'If it ever goes wrong,' he says, 'I have *this*.' That was his plan early on, and he stuck to it. He's in his early thirties and by the age of forty he could be a spent force in darts (although I hope not – he's still a joy to watch at close quarters), but whatever happens he'll still have a home. Plenty of others are savvy, too – Gerwyn Price (the new world champion and world number one) has been sensible; Phil Taylor's had his troubles with divorce but he's looked after his money.

I sit somewhere between the frugal players and the big spenders. I don't like to end the year with less than I started with, but I enjoy being able to buy bits and bobs, and as long as I end the year with a bank balance at or in excess of how things looked on 1 January, I'm fine.

In honesty, 'bits and bobs' does rather understate the situation. I'm always buying stuff. Donna once said to me: 'Wayne, you buy a lot of things, don't you?' I think this was shortly after I went through a two-week spree buying televisions: a new one for the main lounge, plus screens for rooms that had previously been unburdened by televisual delight: one for my office, one for my school of darts, then a big new monitor for the computer.

Another rather more expensive habit involves watch-buying. I excuse this horological expenditure on the basis that I never want to be broke or go totally skint, but accumulating what I'll describe here as 'a few watches' represents 100 per cent justified spending because watches have a habit of keeping their value. It's not like I've bought forty grand's worth of sausage meat or a life-size ice sculpture of Vernon Kay.

I appreciate the 'it's an investment' defence is one often favoured by the sort of person who ends up lumbered with an attic full of Beanie Babies twenty years after they went out of fashion, but I like nice watches, I can afford them, and I know that if push comes to shove I can sell them for a decent price.

If not, I'll always be sitting on a couple of quid. Just as long as I actually hang on to them. I've already given a Rolex and an expensive Steve McQueen TAG Heuer to my nephew, and I do worry that if he's anything like I was at that age those two watches are currently in the window of Romford Cash Converters, having been 'converted' into a handful of PlayStation games. I must bring this up the next time we meet.

11.

LEGENDS

There are plenty of great darts players around, but there's a difference between a great darts player and a darting legend. Before Simon Cowell came along and ruined everything with his Saturday-night panto we used to call it 'x factor'. It's nothing you can put your finger on, but it's also a million things at once.

When I was in my teens playing for London Youth, at big events we'd be invited onto the stage to play before the men's game. I suppose looking back we were the warm-up act before the main event, but back then when I was getting on that stage in front of hundreds of people it felt like I was at the centre of the universe. As soon as we were off stage and the proper players came out, that universe reconfigured, and for me it was hard to ignore the gravitational pull of a John Lowe, a Dennis Priestley or, most importantly, an Eric Bristow.

As a teenager Bristow was my sporting idol. And when I say sporting idol, I'm not just talking about darts. More than any footballer, athlete, cricketer or darts player he was the one for me. Bristow was and probably still is the catalyst for so many players to get into the sport.

There's so much I can say about Eric Bristow. He had the lot: the *joie de vivre*, the charisma, the swagger. And I think he had the lot because he knew he was better than the rest – only people who have an inner self-belief, crossed with innate ability, can really swan about like they own the place.

You'll have heard that phrase 'you know when they've walked into a room' – some people are just like that. They might not say anything or do anything, but when you're in their presence they demand respect, and that's the sort of guy Bristow was. Before Eric Bristow, nobody had it. There were darts champions like Leighton Rees, the first world champion in 1978, then John Lowe and Alan Evans, and they were all stars in their own right throughout the 1970s, but when Bristow came along the world of darts changed forever.

Until Bristow the game had been dominated by players who looked like a cross between your milkman, the strange Uncle Clive your mum refused to talk about for reasons she declined to mention, and a disgraced former zoo keeper. And that was just the women players. As far as the public could see, the game had always been played by the sort of rather ill-looking, middle-aged individual who'd be the first to pop their clogs in a disaster movie.

But Eric came along and he looked different. He was still quite young when he first rose to fame, and I'm not overstating the case when I say he was like the Beckham of his time. He looked liked a superstar. He was a young man playing a middle-aged man's game: he was tall, (relatively) slim, and to a ten-year-old Wayne Mardle he felt like he was somehow in reach. He shone a light on the fact that the other darts players were of a generation who could still remember rationing, and looking back it was like seeing Boris Becker smash Wimbledon at the age of seventeen. As a kid I saw Bristow and thought: 'He's not much older than me. I could do this too.' Darts suddenly seemed more accessible than it had before. I thought: 'This is doable.'

But Bristow didn't just look different – he played different, too. He didn't throw like anyone else did; he moved quicker, he threw better, his action was extravagant. For Bristow it wasn't just a matter of chucking a dart at a board. His hand glided back and it moved like nobody's before and nobody's since.

Plus he was box-office dynamite. Darts was already on TV when Bristow came along, but his presence in the game elevated it to the status where darts became part of the national conversation. You could flick through the channels when other players were on the oche, but with Bristow you wouldn't want to miss a moment. Whether you wanted him to win or to lose, you were mesmerised. Of course, whoever he was up against I wanted him to succeed, and most of the time he did – nine times out of ten I was in the winner's camp. He looked better, he *was* better, and all the other players knew it.

I'll never forget the first time I met Bristow, and over the years I refused to let him forget it either. It was 1985, I was twelve, and the event was London vs Lancashire at the Boston Arms in Tufnell Park, Tottenham. Bristow was practising with Bobby Semple, a Scottish darts champion who'd later become a pairs partner of mine, but back then of course neither of them had a clue who I was. Even though I was far younger than all the pros in the room, I'd been playing around adults long enough not to feel out of place or intimidated, so I asked Bobby if I could practise: 'Mr Semple, can I have a throw, please?'

Thinking back I must have been a bit annoying, but it was then that Eric Bristow appeared next to me. This was my moment. Back then, while my mates were reading *Shoot* or *Smash Hits*, my publication of choice was *Darts World* – every month I'd go off down the newsagent and swap 80p for a window into the wonderful world of darts and I'd devour every single page. And as I stood there in that Tottenham boozer a few feet away from my idol for the first time, one particular story from the pages of *Darts World* sprang to mind. Apparently when Bristow first met John Lowe, a player he'd go on to surpass in every possible way, he said: 'You don't know me, do you?' And of course Lowe looked at this upstart and shook his head. 'You soon will', Lowe was told. 'Eric Bristow's the name.'

Such a typical Eric thing to say. Anyway, I now wanted to say the same thing to Eric. I mean, not verbatim – it would have been weird to introduce yourself to Eric Bristow as Eric Bristow. My plan was to use my own name. Without being a dick about it, even at the age of twelve I knew I was better than most. So when Eric had finished throwing, I picked my moment. But as the words started to leave my lips, I realised I was more nervous than I'd initially expected.

'Hi, er, Eric,' I stumbled, 'you don't know me but … you will?'

He looked me up and down. 'What's your name?'

'Wayne.'

'Well, Wayne, I know you now.'

He turned away and carried on throwing. And in my mind I was thinking: 'I said it! I did it! It didn't come out like I wanted it to, but I said it!'

Fast-forward four years and I meet Bristow again. This time he's presenting me with a trophy, after I've won a televised youth event. And as he was handing me the trophy, I reminded him of our first meeting. There was a flash of *something* across his face, like he was somehow judging me. In the years that followed I'd come to realise that Eric had a way of thinking people were talking to him just to talk to 'the superstar Eric Bristow' – after years and years of hangers-on and yes men he'd developed an instinctive bullshit radar. Sixteen-year-old me must have realised what was happening, because I filled him in on the details of where and when we'd met, adding: 'You had the red and white London shirt on.'

I'd obviously passed the test. He looked a bit wistful for a moment, and offered: 'Yeah, that rings a bell.' That's about as good as it got with Bristow. I felt like he heard me and, for the first time, really saw me.

On top of that I had the guy I'd come to view as Mr Darts presenting *me* with a trophy and saying well done. I don't often think about many specific moments in my darting life, and my house is pretty memorabilia-free: if you visited Mardle Mansion (not really a mansion, but I do like alliteration) you'd never guess my sporting past. Put me on *Through the Keyhole* and I'd be either the best or the worst mystery celebrity the show had ever seen. But that moment on stage with Bristow, knowing I'd performed well in front of him as well as my parents, is something I always treasure, and a photo of that exact moment is up on the wall in my home office. (That photograph is the clue they'd eventually have to show on *Through the Keyhole*.)

Though Bristow didn't exactly shower me with love and affection on those first few occasions we met, I grew to accept that I'd got off pretty lightly. Years later I did an exhibition with him and someone said to me: 'Wayne, where do you see yourself in five years?'

Eric chipped in: 'Probably dead, but who cares?'

He was charming, but he was offensive; he was loyal, but he was brutally disgusting. He could say things so unbelievably atrocious you'd never want to talk to him again, then he'd do something where you'd think: 'What a kind person.' From day to day and even hour to hour you simply could not read Eric Bristow. Speak to anyone who knew Eric and they'll tell you stories about the nastiness that appeared out of nowhere, then they'll tell you stories that will leave you in awe of how much of a beautiful human being he could be.

Once, for instance, I remember an exhibition where all the players were in the practice room and someone came up and told us that there was a young kid downstairs who was asking for our autographs. This kid had cerebral palsy and just couldn't get up the stairs. Eric wasn't having it. 'I'm not going down,' he said. 'I don't have time for this, drag him up the stairs.' None of us could believe what we were hearing.

But then there was another time – a similar situation, in fact, at the Circus Tavern for the World Championship. The dad of this young boy in a wheelchair said to Eric: 'Is there any way you can sign my boy's book for me?' Eric obliged.

Then Eric disappeared upstairs and found the rest of the players: the great and the good of the darting world. He got behind them all, like a sheepdog, and basically herded – or shoved – the whole lot downstairs to also sign this boy's autograph album. I remember him bellowing: 'You're not going anywhere until you've signed that kid's book.' After the event Eric found the kid and gave him his shirt, his darts, a hug and a wink. The kid was in tears. His dad was in tears. To be frank, I felt something in my own eye too. Eric was the kid's darting idol, and that kid's dad's darting idol too, and that day Eric went above and beyond to live up to expectations.

His moments of generosity were sometimes more low-key, too. She didn't tell me this until years later, but back in the day my Donna used to smoke and at one particular darts event when I was otherwise engaged there was some fella pestering her for a light, then pestering her more generally, and just being a total nuisance. Eric saw all this happening and intervened. 'You need to just go away, mate,' he said. 'Leave her alone.'

Donna knew Eric's work for the day was done and that he probably wanted to clear off, but Eric waited nearby for nearly an hour until that creep at the bar left, got in his car and drove off. Donna's sure Eric would have stepped in and helped out anybody who looked like they were in trouble.

I understand that on the day Eric passed, 5 April 2018, he'd had a good day. He'd been playing at a Premier League event in Liverpool, and by all accounts he was gentle and polite that day, drinking Guinness and being nice to people. That's how he went out, and that's the Eric I like to remember.

You might say it's ironic that John Lowe, the player with a no-frills, no-nonsense, no-drama approach to darts who was from an earlier generation of darts player and was surpassed in the seventies by Bristow's cocky persona, went on to outlive Eric. Old Stoneface quietly got on with his work, becoming a three-time World Championship winner and a two-time World Masters champion, with a run of twenty-eight World Championship appearances that wasn't beaten until Phil Taylor bagged it in the 2010s.

John's approach to the sport was in total contrast to mine; he was the opposite of a showman, and in fact attempted to get Bobby George banned from the sport when Bobby was revolutionising things with extravagant walk-ons and deafening music. John's approach was, basically: 'None of this has any place in darts, say "Ladies and gentlemen, John Lowe" and get it over with. I'll walk on stage, play my game and walk off again.' John didn't like the way Bobby wanted the game to go, but Bobby got his way. Particularly because in Bobby's corner you had Eric Bristow. Bristow might not have had the cape, but he wanted to show off as well, and once the public had its first taste of showmanship, there was no going back.

But I admire John for standing his ground. Lowe liked things his way – his genius on the oche was that he was meticulous in every way. He always was, and he still is.

I do regret never getting to meet Jocky Wilson. I never came close to regretting the hundreds of games I lost over the years, but I'll always feel sad about never having the opportunity to shake Jocky Wilson by the hand. I've been around top darts players since 1985, yet an audience with Jocky always eluded me; by the time I joined the BDO he'd joined the PDC; then by the time I joined the PDC he'd retired.

And for Jocky, this wasn't the standard darts retirement of knocking the professional life on the head but still popping up for the occasional exhibition or promo opportunity. When Jocky left darts, he really left darts.

He didn't get to make old bones, sadly. He smoked like a chimney and he liked a wee dram, and that was what his days consisted of; he died of a heart disease at the age of just sixty-two. When news of his health problems and financial concerns filtered through the darts community, Eric Bristow tried to organise a PDC benevolent night, but Jocky wasn't interested in taking the money. He was either proud or stubborn or both. He just wanted nothing to do with it. I think Eric took that, and Jocky's subsequent death, as quite a blow – most people think Eric and Jocky hated each other, but Eric was a gentle, principled human being (when he wasn't being a 100 per cent arse) and he'd phone Jocky more than any other human, just to check he was alright.

It's easy to dwell on the end of Jocky's life, but on balance I prefer to think of the highs – a two-time world champion, no less – and some of the more unusual stories I've heard from when he was in his prime. Bobby George is the source of most of these. He tells a rather strange tale of the time when Jocky won the 1982 World Championship and, over the course of that event, he and Bobby had been sharing a hotel room at the Lakeside, the original home of World Darts.

Bear in mind they were both enormous superstars at this point, as close as dartists of that era came to being household names, and the image of them cooped up in the same room like Bert and Ernie off *Sesame Street* might sound quite comical. But it wasn't so enjoyable for Bobby, who noticed a few days in that Jocky wasn't changing his underpants. Jocky insisted they were lucky, and refused to change them until he won. He did eventually put on a clean pair, but that was after seven days. Poor old Bobby. Still, by that point Jocky was the champion of the world.

It's hard to imagine any of the darting world's current legends, from Gary Anderson to Michael van Gerwen, spending seven days in the same undercrackers. The legends I grew up with were often one-man operations, but almost all the professionals have managers now, and though it's hardly a contractual obligation it's fair to expect most management teams will keep an eye on basic personal hygiene.

Of the current lot I'd say it's Michael van Gerwen whose management are the best in the world – not only do they keep him away from the nonsense of social media, but they've got him to the stage where wherever he happens to be, and wherever in the world he wants to find himself, they lay on everything that's needed to make his movements as enjoyable and stress-free as possible. He's treated like a big name DJ wherever he goes, and taking away all that unnecessary stress, protecting the asset, means Michael can focus on his job: winning darts matches.

These days all the current and future legends put on a show, but that wasn't always the case and Bobby George's impact on the game really can't be overstated. He was the first true showman in darts. With his bulging muscles, square shoulders and a toothy grin so dazzling you could stick him on a cliff and decommission every lighthouse in a ten-mile radius, Bobby always looked like a cross between Mr Universe, an Olympic weightlifter and a secondhand car dealer.

Bobby is a whole lot of human being. He was thirty years old before he took up darts but didn't waste any time and was winning major tournaments within a matter of years. He's never been a man for half measures, on the oche or off it. And he's the guy who brought a real sense of showmanship to darts through a combination of wanting to entertain crowds and also, just as importantly, wanting to entertain himself. As I mentioned, the whole walk-on music thing was down to Bobby back in the eighties – he wanted it, he got it, and by the nineties he was walking on with the cape and candelabra like Liberace. He didn't care what people thought. He just wanted people to enjoy themselves.

His nicknames included Bobby Dazzler and, more commonly, the King of Bling, the latter best illustrated by the fact that by the 2000s he was living in a sprawling Essex mansion he called George Hall. I'm quite close with Bobby and he often says to me: 'Your career's mirroring mine.' But I can't see myself ever building a brilliantly ludicrous seventeen-bedroom manor in twelve acres of grounds that take in two fishing lakes and an outdoor kitchen. Bobby used to joke about the scale of the place: it was so big, he said, that he and his wife Marie hardly ever saw each other, and he designed it all himself.

As for whether my career's mirroring his, my comparatively abysmal list of wins speaks for itself, but he might have a point when it comes to the showmanship. In the animal world there's a thing called imprinting, where newborns form a bond with the earliest thing they see. Research has shown a baby duck will bond with literally anything, even an inanimate object: whether it's the nearest human, a football or a Twix wrapper, that duckling will think it's found its mother. I don't know if that's what happened when the King of Bling became the first darting superstar I ever met, back at the Romford Co-Op Club, but that would certainly explain the rather exuberant personality I later developed as a darts player.

'That's Bobby George', my dad said, the first time I clocked him.

'I know', I replied. 'And I want to play him.'

According to Bobby – and he mentions this to me about fifty times a year, because he only lives twenty minutes down the road from my own house and we're always bumping into each other – the first time I went up to him, I tugged on his trouser leg and said: 'Me play you! Me play you!'

Now far be it from me to question the recall of the King of Bling, but you need to bear in mind that by this point I was twelve years old and capable of structuring a complete sentence – probably with greater panache than I can today. In addition to that, I was the best part of five feet eight inches tall. I was not, in other words, a toddler. At that age I wasn't even drinking, and that's the only other reason I'd have been on the floor and incapable of coherent speech. But while there's some dispute over what I said to Bobby, we both remember exactly what he said when I asked for a game: 'No.'

Externally I might have been big for my age, but inside I was crushed. When he explained that if he played me he'd end up having to play every other bloke in the pub, it sounded like he was making an excuse; and it was some years before I gained some notoriety myself and found that I'd often be asked for a game when I was out and about. When that started happening I realised how right Bobby had been to turn me down.

I've been 'given away' in charity raffles and auctions over the years; people will pay over a grand to play a game of darts against me, but it's really nothing to do with money. What Bobby George knew that day, and what I'd learn decades later, is that if you say yes to one person, you need to say yes to everyone in the pub, and someone's always going to miss out.

The happy ending, of course, is that as the decades flew by I came to know Bobby as a friend: it was Bobby, of course, who gave me the Hawaii 501 nickname, and these days we live so close to each other that we're as likely to bump into each other in Halfords as at a major darts event. And if there's any true measure of a legend it's that they still sparkle and amaze when you see them comparing competing brands of screenwash.

12.

FAME AND FANS

I opened this book with a story about accidentally throwing a dart through the hand of a fan (in Rhyl, of all places) and being rewarded with a smile and a thank you. I always think of that story when I'm asked what fame is like, and if the tale of that Rhyl debacle tells you one thing it's this: fame is strange. Under normal Saturday-night pub circumstances, the act of chucking a dart through someone's hand would likely result in the involvement of the local constabulary. But because I was famous, I got a smile and a thank-you.

Darts would be nothing without its fans. When I was still competing at a professional level I'd find that during the breaks, while the other player might go off and get a drink or sandwich, or for a rub down to alleviate the pressure I'd put on them, I couldn't help staying on stage, interacting with the crowd and, perhaps, doing my best to get them on *my* side. 'Come on!' I'd yell into the crowd. 'Cheer for me!'

As we learned during the lockdown livestreams, darts can be competitive and meaningful in an empty room, but we need a crowd alongside us to make the sport truly exciting.

Without them the sport simply does not exist. I had some terrible games of darts over the years, but I never felt those times were truly worthless because I had paying punters all around me, and almost without exception they could lift even the darkest of moods. They create the atmosphere. They *are* the atmosphere.

The fans absolutely do not get the recognition they deserve, but going all the way back to the seventies they've been a fundamental part of what's made darts so big. I've had nights where I couldn't have hit a cow's arse with a banjo, but still fans come up to me afterwards: they want a chat, they want you to meet their mates, they still consider you part of their world, even if you've played a stinker of a game. They tell me how much I give them through my work in and around darts, but the truth is darts fans give me more than they'll ever know.

The scene's changing, though. Darts has evolved in the last twenty years, and with the explosion in darts' popularity there's also been a shift in who's coming to big events. Bob Anderson once said that the darts fans back in the day were simply players themselves from local pubs and clubs; nowadays you'll just as often find a World Championship audience filled with people who want to come out for a party and have never even held a dart, let alone thrown one.

I'm hardly innocent when it comes to whipping crowds into a frenzy, but one thing you won't hear much of at a modern darts event is the sound of … well, nothing. Looking back a few years, the silence that would descend on a room when you were about to take an important throw made things feel so important. Straight away the significance of a moment was heightened to a level that just hadn't been in the room before: it was if you were suddenly alone in a different building. As you were drawing your arm back you'd know: 'This is important.' Even with a thousand others around you there was a sense of intimacy, although I suppose there's always something rather intimate about being drenched in the sweat of a thousand people as it drips from a low ceiling.

These days, in larger venues, that intimacy's really hard to recreate – and the silences are long gone. When players go for an important shot, the noise actually increases, the rowdiness builds, and it's not even always a positive noise because some people even start booing. Once upon a time, audiences would self-police: a crowd member could yell 'WAHEEYYY!!' when someone was throwing a dart and they'd be chucked out. Now everyone's at it.

A whole lot can change in twenty years. I remember when I was starting out I'd see the same faces at all the televised events: the World Championship, then the World Matchplay, then the World Grand Prix, then Bolton for the Open, then the exhibitions. Afterwards they'd perhaps want a signature, or a nice photo with you and their family. Darts fans now feel more remote; many still come to the big events, but just as many are content to consume the sport from the comfort of their own home, buying merch from websites and chatting over social media. They're still connected, but where once they wanted to actually be there with you, now they feel they don't need physical proximity in order to know you.

Fan-attended events are still a big deal, though, and I've been party to some rather unusual encounters over the years.

Believe me when I say you never know what you're going to take away from an encounter with a darts fan.

Case in point: I was booked for a pub event in Wales a couple of years back, and all night, no matter who I spoke to, there was one question I was constantly asked: 'Have you met Bob yet?' Everybody was very keen for me to meet this mysterious Bob. 'Go and find him!' 'Get Bob!' 'Bob's quite a character!' The night continued, I played against a couple of locals, drinks flowed and eventually, *finally*, the mysterious Bob made himself known.

He sticks out his hand to shake mine and, bearing in mind this was pre-COVID times when you'd willingly shake someone's hand without first inspecting it for mange, I happily grabbed his hand – and his entire arm fell off.

'Don't worry,' he grinned. 'It happens all the time!'

Shock turned to horror turned to total mortification, and the entire pub roared with laughter. Turns out Bob had lost his actual arm a few years back and the old 'prosthetic limb falling off' routine was something of a party trick.

'Hilarious, isn't it?' Bob offered. You may already have surmised that Bob, by this point in the evening, was as pissed as a fart.

I, meanwhile, had sobered up rather quickly. 'I'll be honest with you, Bob,' I replied while trying not to laugh, 'this is a little outside my comfort zone.'

Next thing I knew, the entire pub was chanting 'THROW A DART WITH IT!!!' as Bob waved one arm around using the other. Once the shock subsided I'd rather warmed to the hand, but I did politely decline throwing with it because it felt like a line would be crossed if it hadn't been already, but somewhere on the internet there's still a photo of me wielding Bob's prosthetic arm with a dart stuck through its hand. I don't know what it is about me, Wales, and darts going through people's hands, but I'd suggest that if you ever see me in the Valleys you give me a wide berth because there's no telling how our encounter might pan out.

My main takeaway from The Bob Incident is that if you're out in public and a fan holds something out, check what you're dealing with before you shake it. And that's a lesson that stood me in good stead at a subsequent event during which, and there's no delicate way of putting this, I ended up signing a penis.

I should probably elaborate. For instance, if I explain that I was in Holland, the story may already be starting to make more sense. I was booked at an exhibition and a guy appears: a tanned, beefed-up Adonis of a human being who'd turn any head – female, male, gay, straight – simply by walking into a room. Turned out, according to my new Dutch friends, this chap was a famous male porn star who also happened to love darts. Later on he'd had a few drinks, we'd been entertaining the crowd, and to be fair I wasn't exactly sober. Inevitably his penis came up, so to speak. Eventually, he went: 'You should sign my penis!'

I laughed of course, quipped that I'd just grab a pen, and jokingly made as if to reach round to my jacket pocket to get a Sharpie. By the time I've turned back this gentleman had unfurled – and there really is no other way of describing the ceremony of that moment – an appendage of truly gargantuan proportions. 'Wayne', he said solemnly. 'Sign my penis.'

Andy Fordham was sitting across from us. We exchanged a glance. Andy simply shrugged, as if to say, 'When in Holland ...' And so, crowd-pleaser that I am, I popped my signature on there. In fact there was so much room that Andy ended up putting his own name down as well. Our full names, too, with room to spare. It's a shame it didn't all take place in Thailand, to be honest – there would have been ample space for local legend Thanawat Gaweenuntawong to get his signature on the end if he'd fancied.

A note here on signing items: if you're thinking of seriously getting into darts, you'll need to give your scribble some thought. When I first started out I was signing stuff using the signature I was also using for cheques, a practice that stopped abruptly when someone pointed out that this wasn't, perhaps, the most sensible situation from a security point of view. So I developed a proper autograph: 'Wayne Hawaii 501 Mardle'.

That was shortened during a particularly gruelling afternoon in 2004. I was asked to signed 501 dartboards at an invitational event – I lasted twenty minutes before it had been shortened to 'Wayne Hawaii 501'. Roland 'The Tripod' Scholten earned my respect that day. Faced with 501 dartboards he began by signing 'Roland' on one side then 'Scholten' on the other, followed by '180', followed by '2004' then, quite spectacularly, a smiley face. The whole thing was absolutely ridiculous. By the end I was simply scrawling 'Wayne', but Roland's autograph didn't change across 501 dartboards. They say darts is a game that requires willpower, strength and determination, and Scholten earned his stripes that day.

The Dutch penis moment was a strange affair, all told, but a brilliant illustration of one of my very favourite things about darts: the accessibility of players to the fans who support the game. The fact that the sport is relatively small, in terms of the number of people playing, plays a big role here, as does the culture of exhibitions which means small pubs and clubs can hire well-known darts players, world champions among them, to turn up and do their stuff for an evening's entertainment.

There are certain sports in which the sportsperson has little to no interaction with those who are so important to the game. Football's one of them: professional players are absolutely shielded from the paying punter, the audience, the fan. There are times when they're not even allowed to be touched or high-fived by the audience who idolise them, and I find that quite sad. You can't imagine Ronaldo turning up at the Burnley Miners to hang out with supporters, or pulling off Bob's arm in a Welsh boozer. And you certainly can't imagine him turning up with an entourage of less than twenty people, when my own MO is to rock up on my own, or at most with Donna in tow.

I think anyone with a public profile remembers the first time they were recognised while out and about. For me, it's still as clear as day. It was long before I turned pro, but I'd started making a bit of a name for myself; I was on a train to Romford on the way home from work and this commuter sitting next to me leaned over and said: 'Wayne, I just want to say I enjoyed watching you in the World Championship.'

It meant so much that he'd made the effort to start that conversation with me. But I also realised for the first time what being famous (or at least *darts* famous) really meant. It means people knowing who you are, and what you do, even when you know nothing about them. It's an odd one to get your head around, and you never know when or where you might be recognised.

Not so long ago I was in a discount clothing store in Clacton-on-Sea – we were out and about, the weather turned and Donna needed an emergency hoodie. I'd been in the store about ten seconds and I heard, being bellowed across the bras: 'HAWAII FIVE-O! WHAT ARE YOU DOING IN THIS SHITHOLE?' I didn't know what was most alarming: the fact that I'd been identified in among shelves of underwear or the fact that the fella shouting about the 'shithole' was doing so from behind the sales desk.

Then there was the time I was having an absolute shocker in one of the Premier Leagues and decided I needed to get away from the world of darts, so Donna and I phoned a travel agent and left that afternoon for Tenerife. Tenerife, of course, not being well known for its darting scene. The following morning I was having breakfast in a local café and this fella walked past, saw me, doubled back and shouted at me: 'You cost me fifty quid the other night!' Then he walked off. Half an hour later I'd just about got my head back together when he walked past again. He looked me up and down and went: 'Shouldn't you be practising?' He was wearing a Manchester United shirt, make of which what you will.

All that said, I can hardly complain if people do stroll up to me and strike up conversation, even if that conversation is rather one-sided and based on the outcome of an unsuccess-ful bet. The side of myself I've always tried to put across on stage and in front of the camera is the approachable, easygoing part of my nature. From the start I wanted my image to revolve around having fun, being colourful and being accessible and personable. I want people to think of me and maybe smile.

When you see how some other players present themselves you can see the difference. Hop on over to the Target Darts website and every picture looks like they've walked out of a week in an interrogation room and straight into a Scandinavian crime drama. They're dark, and moody, and they're not smiling; it's serious and industrial and every single one of those players looks like the last person you'd approach for a selfie unless you wanted your phone snatched off you and lobbed at the nearest wall.

Ask *me* for a selfie, however, and you'll have a very different experience. As long as you stick to some very strict rules. Selfies actually took a little while to catch on in the darts world – we weren't exactly One Direction, and as the great Eric Bristow once noted: 'You cannot beat a fucking Kodak.' But in 2021 they're here to stay, so it's worth laying out my rules.

I'm more than happy to stop for a picture with anyone, but I expect the phone to be unlocked, the right way up, switched to the camera app and ready to go. I know we're all coming to terms with changing technology, but let's be prepared. The edict is this: in and out in eight seconds or it's not happening. I might also add that asking for a selfie then getting someone else to take the picture renders the picture very much not a selfie at all, and I object to non-selfie-selfies on a fundamental level.

I'll add a word of warning here to future darting superstars: examine the *mise en scène* before agreeing to a photo with a fan. Not so long ago someone asked for a photo when I'd just come out of a pub toilet cubicle and when I checked the photo afterwards I couldn't believe what I was seeing. 'Let's try again, shall we?' I suggested, deleting the photo. 'And this time let's try to make sure there's nobody doing Class As behind us.' The original photo had captured, in all their glory, two fellas doing cocaine off a toilet seat. I appreciate I'm well known for my energy on stage, but I didn't want anyone getting the wrong idea.

So selfies are fine, autographs are all good, a nice chat when I'm collecting a new drill in Homebase is very much encouraged. But sometimes the notion of fandom takes a rather more extreme turn.

There have been a number of stalkers on the darts scene over the years: they start by turning up at events, then figuring out which hotels to book rooms in so they'll see players at breakfast, then discovering which pubs and clubs players go to in order to relax. Some of these people have penetrated the inner circle (not as painful as it sounds), and one or two of the female fans have even gone on to start relationships with players. The idea of developing a fixation on someone you've never met is strange at the best of times, but also – and I hope no darts players reading this take offence – more often than not the targets of these obsessions are not exactly what you'd call a catch.

I'd include myself in that, of course. To give you an idea of how much effort can go into it for so little potential reward, I found myself being accosted a few years back after an event in Scotland. A woman fifteen years younger than me, single or happy to be thought of as such, offered to get me a drink and became quite overpowering quite quickly. She mentioned that she knew where I was staying because she'd got that information out of someone else. I made it clear that I was married, said goodbye and that was that.

A week later I was in Germany for a different event, and she was in the front row. 'What a strange coincidence', I thought. Later that day I was in a restaurant with Barney, Phil and the organiser; I looked over, and there she was at another table, sitting by herself. I mentioned how peculiar this was and the organiser said: 'Oh dear, she was asking earlier and I told her which hotel you're staying at.'

Sure enough, at the hotel bar later that evening, she turned up, plonked herself next to me, and announced: 'I'm staying at this hotel too, but I'm willing not to use my room, if you know what I mean.' I'm not well known for subtlety myself, but even I thought this was bold. I quietly made it clear, again, that whatever she had in mind would not be happening, and that was the end of that.

Except two weeks later I was in Belfast for a tournament, and who did I see in the front row? You've guessed it. I got back to the hotel, had a nightcap with the organiser and of course there once again was this woman. Again, she pulled over a chair and sat with us. By this point I'd had enough. I stood up, announced 'I'm not going to sleep with you', and went to bed. I must confess I felt pretty guilty. Even though I'd been rattled by the whole thing and she'd obviously crossed a line, I still didn't like the feeling that I'd upset her. But I needed it to be clear that she'd wasted her journey, and shouldn't book any similar journeys in the future.

The next morning I was chatting with another player, who'd seen the whole thing unfold the previous evening. I expressed how bad I was feeling about having upset someone who was, at the end of the day, just a fan of my playing.

'I wouldn't worry,' he said. 'She went off with the event organiser.'

It might sound weird, but reality-check moments like that are actually really important if you find yourself getting lost in the idea of 'fame', or too caught up in what being famous really means. I don't think anyone can really predict how they'd adapt to fame until they're actually in the moment.

Generally speaking I feel like I've handled fame pretty well. For instance I've never ever, ever played the 'do you know who I am?' card. Largely because I've seen the humiliation that occurs when someone does try it, only to be met with a shrug and a shake of the head. But I'll admit there's been the occasional ego-driven wobble, and there was a particular point in the mid-2000s when the idea of fame did go to my head a little.

I started getting serious TV time in the 2000s, and by 2005 I'd grown used to adulation coming my way, at least in darting environments. I've spoken to other players about this since, and I know I wasn't alone in feeling that things were getting a bit out of hand across the entire sport as darts became more and more mainstream. A rising tide lifts all boats, they say – and it was easy to act like a luxury yacht when in actual fact you were a £14.99 Argos dinghy. Holsten Pils used to sponsor the Premier League and I'd regularly ask them to send me a few cases whenever I'd have a barbecue coming up. That's not the sort of thing I'd do now: back then I thought fame and importance were interchangeable, but now I know the two concepts are totally independent. You can be important without being famous and, more significantly, you can be famous but that doesn't make you important.

It takes a while to come to that realisation. I remember once or twice asking for certain bottles of wine or food backstage at events, purely to be awkward. There was one game in particular, in Doncaster, when I was still a KFC freak and I decided I wanted a bucket. I remember wandering around, going: 'Can someone go and get me a KFC?' It might sound like a small thing compared with some of the diva demands you hear about from global superstars, but I remember how wrong it sounded coming out of my mouth, and it haunted me for weeks afterwards. It was a bit of a wake-up call: I was behaving as if I was the most important person in the building, when I really wasn't – at best I was a tiny cog in a huge wheel.

Also, I never even got the bargain bucket, which I suppose should have been as clear an indication as any of where I really stood that day. Either way, it was a wake-up call. So if you were there that day and refused my demands for a KFC: my most sincere thanks.

13.

TRAVEL

You can divide the planet's entire population into two distinct groups: those who arrive at an airport as gates are being called, and those who choose to give the whole ordeal at least three hours longer than necessary. These two groups of people should not cohabit, it's unwise for them to mingle, and in an ideal world these two subsections of humanity would never even know the other exists.

Me? I'm a three-hours merchant. I just can't bear the idea of being late. I'm big on punctuality in all areas of life and I hold myself to the standards I expect of others. I know that if I'm late for a flight I could miss whichever engagement someone expects me to be at, and while it might only be a darts exhibition at a bar in Germany or at a club in Holland, that one night for me might be the focal point of someone else's entire calendar. They might have been looking forward to this for weeks. Imagine: they could have cancelled their wedding in order to make it along. Also imagine: they may have tattooed my face across their back in anticipation of meeting me. And there's no way I can know what might impede my journey. Maybe the

M25 is shut! Could there be an overturned cow on the A12? It's impossible to predict.

There's only been one flight-missing incident where I've had any sort of defence and that was back in the day when I was due to appear at a tour event in Nuland, Holland, and I was at Stansted airport with the PDC press officer, Dave Allen, the chief executive of the PDC, Matt Porter, and some other players. We were all chatting about the inept ranking system and how it worked for some and not for others, and we got so engrossed in this fascinating topic that we totally missed the flight. If you're with the chief exec it's okay. That's my story and, even today, I'm sticking to it.

So that's why I arrive at airports hours before I need to.

All of which may sound fairly convincing, and there's an element of truth in there somewhere, but putting manners to one side for a moment I'll be completely honest with you and admit that the main reason I get to airports early is that a few years ago I discovered the joy of the private lounge.

I mean no disrespect to Mardle Towers, but two hours I spend at home is two hours I can't spend in an airport lounge, and I'm fairly certain airport lounges represent the greatest innovation in the transportation of sentient lifeforms since that first fish flopped out of the sea and decided to grow legs, 385 million years ago last Thursday.

They say you never forget your first lounge (and by 'they' I mean 'people happy to throw a load of cash at what they tell themselves is a free croissant'). My own first experience of a lounge was on the way home from an event in Vegas; I'd been away for three weeks, I was totally beat, I was sick of people, and I wanted to get away. The price of admission was $30 and beyond those tinted doors I found the promised land of on-tap drinks, a running buffet, and comfortable seating. That seating! There were *chaises-longues* and leather Chesterfields as far as the eye could see.

Bear in mind, this was only about a decade ago – I'd finished my professional career. I instantly wondered why I'd deprived my derrière of such furniture-rich utopias for so many years. The answer was: I'd rarely travel on my own, and more often than not I'd been hanging around with other players: Andy Jenkins, Colin Monk, Kevin Painter, Colin Lloyd and Steve Maish. Chaps – I fantasised – who were either in a financial tight spot or, more likely, total skinflints. But travelling without them I was free. Free to pay for a priority lounge pass. Free to sit in a posh chair. Free to achieve a state of pastry-aided airport zen. Free to be the me I always knew I could be.

The only real problem with lounges is that more and more people are now succumbing to the Siren's call of the fruit platter, meaning that lounges are gradually becoming busier. There will soon come a time when it's more relaxing not to be in a lounge than it is to be in one, but until the global lounge scene crosses that event horizon you should know I take my quiet very seriously to the point where I think it might even be a bit of a problem.

There's a lounge in Cologne where there's only ever four or five people in there. (Not the same four or five people – that would be strange.) I always make a point of arriving extra early in Cologne. I'll look airports up in advance to see if there are multiple lounges and, if there are, I'll look up reviews to find out which are the best. Sometimes at exhibitions I'll give an event organiser my darts and a Jiffy bag to be sent to my home, just so I can go for an extra-long sleep in a lounge's massage chairs.

That darts-in-the-post trick is one worth knowing. Whether you're going to use a lounge or not, it's always worth remembering that when you're a darts player you are, to all intents and purposes, travelling with a deadly weapon. In the old days we used to just pop our darts in a coat pocket and get on the plane with them. Mind you, those were also the days when it was totally permissible to light up a fag as you hurtled through the sky in a tin bucket loaded with aviation fuel, so I'm not suggesting progress is a bad thing. But checking in your darts with your luggage carries the same risk as checking in *anything*.

One time when I was playing in Gibraltar in the mid-2000s we arrived at the tiny airport with its one luggage carousel and after an hour of waiting it became crystal clear that my belongings, including the clothes I was due to play in and the darts I'd been due to play with, would not be plopping onto the conveyor belt.

I said to the helpdesk: 'I'm here for business and my business is in that bag.'

'It's still at Gatwick,' they said. 'It'll be here on Monday.'

'So will I – checking in to go home again.'

The upshot of all this was that I had to race to the hotel everyone was staying at and run around like a madman trying to find someone who was using 22-gram Bristows, or something in a similar ballpark, eventually settling on Chris Mason, who agreed to let me borrow his darts. It was very kind of him, particularly as I ended up getting further than Chris in the tournament, although I suppose he took some solace in the fact that my romp to a quarter-final spot was executed in the t-shirt and shorts I'd bought from the hotel gift shop and I probably looked like the kid at school who'd been sent to the lost property box and forced to play rugby in pants and a blouse after forgetting his PE kit.

To be fair to the helpdesk at the airport my stuff did, as promised, turn up on the Monday. I picked it up, wheeled it across the airport for thirty seconds, then checked it straight back in again for my flight home.

I could hardly complain. I mean I did complain, at some length, but the point is I'm hardly in a position to criticise someone else for losing things. I've lost track of the number of sunglasses, phones, chargers and sets of keys I've mislaid over the years. In the seventies there was an episode of Roald Dahl's *Tales of the Unexpected* TV series called 'Lamb to the Slaughter' wherein a housewife bashed her dickhead husband to death with a frozen leg of lamb, then cooked it and ate the evidence. That's generally regarded as the high-water mark of weapon disposal, but I see your leg of lamb and I raise you this: strangle a man with a phone charging cable, then give that phone charger to a darts player. It'll be gone without a trace within ten minutes.

Of course, none of the baggage loss would a problem if there were enough money in darts to support the lifestyle I'm sure you'll agree I totally deserve. A lifestyle enjoyed by professional footballers, for instance, who seem to get everywhere by private jet. But that would be a severe financial jolt for darts players – a few of us would have to club together, and even then we'd still be in the bracket of Definitely Cannot Afford to be Cavorting Around in a Private Jet.

I've investigated, of course. I've done the numbers. Certain places are just a real ballache to get to. Cognac in France, for instance, is a mammoth trek involving various trains, buses and taxis. A few years back Roger, a friend of mine, and I were looking to get there, so I said I'd look at a private chartered flight. I soon realised it was going to cost us the best part of £7,000 each to pull it off. I did the whole 'justifying it to myself' thing and I did a pretty convincing job.

For a start, the regular flights would have been £300 anyway, so the cost of the private jet would only really have been £6,700. Also, all the waiting and check-in malarkey would have been eliminated from my journey, saving time, and time is money, so let's say we're now down to £5,500. The jet included refreshments, which I might have paid for at an airport – and there's always the chance I might have stocked up on underwear in duty-free while bored, and that wouldn't happen on a private airstrip, so now we're down to £5,200. In fact, let's round it down and call it £5,000. This was my thought process, and I was quite pleased with it. I hadn't even set foot on the jet and I'd already saved £2,000. 'Imagine how much money I could save if I took a private jet every week.'

There are times in life when we're facing a dilemma and the kindest thing we can do for ourselves is to slightly separate our consciousness from our physical entity; to imagine that we rise, spiritually, above our own body in order to impartially observe our behaviours and examine the scene playing out before our eyes; and to acknowledge what this aerial view allows us to see. And in that moment, I knew what I saw: a twat, who was going to end up flying RyanAir.

And yes, you'd better believe I have a favourite seat on RyanAir flights. Airlines have plenty of regulations, but I have strict rules of my own when it comes to flying. If you're 'of a certain age' you may recall a time when you'd rock up at the airport, ask for a window seat and hope for the best. I think we can all agree those were dark, harrowing times and while the internet has lumbered humanity with a number of negatives – wild and damaging conspiracy theories, the near collapse of democracy and unspeakable horrors on the dark web – I'd argue that's all vastly outweighed by how easy it now is for me to book the most pleasant seat on a RyanAir flight.

2F. That's the one. That beautiful seat. I'm becoming slightly aroused as I even type those two digits. I'm picturing the scene now: there's a wall in front of me, and a window to my right. Nobody passes me, hinders me or touches me. I can read, I can sleep, I can watch a film if I choose. What's that sound? Ding ding, it's the drinks trolley, and it's coming to me first. I need the bathroom? No problem: the small amount of extra legroom means I can simply stand up and get there, without having to clamber giraffe-like over the seats of other passengers.

They say an Englishman's home is his castle, but this particular Englishman makes his own home wherever he lays his hat, and that's seat 2F, even though I don't ordinarily travel with a hat. (Note to EasyJet flyers: the closest equivalent on your standard orange airbus is 1F – you won't find a wall in front, but everything else is exactly what you need.)

You may be looking at those seat numbers thinking: 'Ooh, get *her* in Premium Economy.' And that's pretty much my inner monologue when I'm booking flights: GET ME IN PREMIUM ECONOMY. I'm lucky that sponsors have paid for some of my flights and that even when they haven't, I've still been able to afford that little extra luxury, but really it all comes down to legroom. I'm six foot one-and-a-half – that half is very important for my ego – and the thought of being uncomfortable for ten hours on my way to Vegas is not a pleasant one.

Also: I'm an athlete! Well, a sportsman, anyway. You wouldn't expect any other sportsman to be crammed into a tiny seat, unless they were literally Steve Cram, and even he's six foot one so I can't imagine he'd be happy about the situation either.

When darts players are travelling en masse we tend to keep ourselves to ourselves on short-haul flights, and there's only one occasion when I can remember being a nightmare passenger – on the way back from the Open in Germany back in 1997, when I was right at the start of my darting travels. I'd sampled rather too much Riesling the night before and couldn't contain myself, meaning that the sick bags were deployed shortly after lift-off.

On longer trips things can get boring, and you must never underestimate the lengths a bored darts player will go to in order to keep themselves amused. On one flight a few years back Alan Warriner, now Warriner-Little, who was world number one at that point and a hell of a player, found himself sitting next to Steve Brown, a Londoner, a big guy, and the owner of some of the most ludicrously thick spectacles you've ever seen – to you or me, putting on his glasses would be like attempting to see life through a couple of Fox's Glacier Mints.

Anyway Warriner has something of a devilish side at the best of times, and the tedium of a transatlantic flight must have ignited something particularly childish in him because he waited until his bespectacled companion was asleep, spread butter all over Steve's glasses, strapped himself back in, and screamed so loudly that Steve burst to life, immediately decided he'd gone blind, and started screaming his own head off, waking up the rest of the cabin in the process.

I've been known to wail on flights myself. Back in 2006, when Donna and I were on our way to Johannesburg for a darts event, we popped on a film and I found it so emotional that I ended up crying like I'd never cried before. To say I was hysterical is putting it mildly – at one point Donna had to tell me to calm down, but she was in no better state. The pair of us were inconsolable. Neither of us could have predicted that outcome when we'd pressed play on *Million Dollar Baby*.

In my defence, heightened emotion on aeroplanes is a well-documented phenomenon. Research commissioned by Virgin Atlantic a few years back revealed that over half of their passengers got overly emotional on planes, with nearly half of all men admitting to burying themselves in blankets to hide their crying from other passengers.

When it comes to events in the UK I'll usually drive. Historically the meaning of 'I'll drive' is that I'll have asked Donna to do the driving, but while writing this book I managed to pass my driving test so these days you might find me behind the wheel. Back in the day, though, there's no doubt whatsoever that for a long time the greatest motorway in the UK was the M1. I'd go so far as to say that stretch of road was magnificent – an effortless and iconic strip of motorway that brought joy to my life every time I used it. This, of course, was before the 'improvements'.

(Other things that have been made worse by improvements: Ribena after the sugar tax, which I support as a general concept but not when it messes with a legendary blackcurrant beverage; that time in 1993 when they did a new version of the *EastEnders* theme that ruined the doof-doofs and incensed the nation so intensely that it was only on air for eleven months; the light fitting in my front room which I did my best to fix and, well, let's just say Donna had called in an electrician within twenty-four hours.)

Now the M1's been ruined, there's no legitimately brilliant motorway in the UK, partly because of nationwide 'improvements' and partly because there are so many cars on the road, the latter meaning that just one accident can wreck a motorway for hours.

Not so long ago I left Essex at 10am for an exhibition in Burnley that evening, and by 9pm – eleven hours later! – we'd managed less than eighty miles. For the entire time I was stuck in that unexplained gridlock I could picture two hundred people turning up at Burnley Working Men's Club along with the MC, caterers and security, and finding Wayne Mardle nowhere to be seen. I was giving the organisers constant updates, but those updates were basically 'still not moving, no idea why'. In the end we had to just accept it wasn't going to happen and decided to go home, but traffic in the other direction was terrible too. We got home at 4am: we'd been gone eighteen hours and we'd achieved precisely nothing. I later discovered the problem had been a large spillage of olive oil – if I'd had some lemon juice and mustard in the car with me I'd have been laughing, but I try not to dwell on what might have been. As the song says, *je vinaigrette rien*.

While I'm on the topic of motorways, I should take a moment to cover the country's best motorway services. I've always been partial to Corley on the M6, which used to be my favourite when we were going north-west to Wigan and Blackpool. But these days we use the A1 bit more and, let me tell you, Peterborough Services is a slice of heaven at Junction 17.

They are absolutely out of this world. The whole thing's laid out in a circle, so wherever you are you can turn your head and see everything around you. Visiting Peterborough Services is the closest I'll ever get to being an owl. The first time I went in there I found myself spinning on the spot, like Trigger looking for Del Boy at the bar after he's fallen through it. I was overwhelmed by the multi-sensory joy of M&S, Zen Noodles, WH Smith and toilets blurring into one beautiful image.

And the chairs? All I can say is: wow. Those chairs are soft bucket chairs. They're not your hard robust 'these will last for decades' chairs. They're catering for the customer and it shows – you can totally imagine local Peterborough youths making a day of it at that place. I've just realised I've hit the age where I praise comfortable seating at motorway services, but anyway: the UK service-station ranking is Peterborough, then Corley, then after that I'm not interested.

On reaching my destination I've found that my hotel requirements have changed over the years. Back in the day I followed other darts players a lot and that would always mean one thing: Premier Inn. Nowadays, I only stay in some Holiday

Inns and, more often, Travelodges. The reason for my switch? They accept dogs, which means I can travel with my two boys, Sherlock and Watson. These days, hotels not being dog-friendly is something of a dealbreaker for me.

If you've ever heard anyone claim that darts is the new rock'n'roll, I must point out that there's one key area in which the two endeavours differ: I have never thrown a hotel telly out of the window. But that doesn't mean I haven't caused some damage to A/V equipment over the years. Which is to say, while I may not have tossed a telly into a swimming pool, I've dropped one or two. You see a lot of cricketers and golfers practising their swing wherever they happen to be, and darts players are similar. Maybe you'll wake up at 6am and think: 'I'll have a throw for five minutes.' This involves erecting a stand and having a throw, but I've so often found that it's necessary to move furniture in order to make room for an erection and that'll invariably lead to TVs balanced precariously where TVs should absolutely not be balanced or, simply, being dropped on the floor.

All accidental, of course, but if you're up for causing some deliberate damage in a hotel room I can heartily recommend the Citywest hotel about twenty-five miles outside Dublin – to the west of the city, as it happens.

There also happens to be a rather nice golf club attached to the hotel, which I'd generally avoid when I was a player in an attempt to reduce the risk of blisters, but now I'm simply commentating I'm down on the fairway as often as I can be. And when I'm in my room I'll do some practice shots. The curtains are so heavy that you can whack a golf ball at them without much concern, but while the windows have remained intact during my visits, the rooms' smoke alarms have not, sadly, been so lucky when I've been doing a full swing. On one occasion an alarm ended up in dozens of pieces on the floor, but I've learned not to make excuses. The next morning you simply tell reception: 'I'm so sorry, I was practising my golf swing and your smoke alarm got in the way.' They've never charged me, so if there's an inner rock star you've always been hoping to express, please do make a reservation at the Citywest, and fill your boots.

My final piece of travel advice, whether you're a future darts pro or simply someone who doesn't want to end up in an unexpected country: check your itinerary, then check it again, and don't trust your phone.

A couple of years back I had a call: 'Wayne, are you free on Friday, May 12th? We'd like to book you for an exhibition in Leeds.' I checked my diary – I was in Rotherham the night before, so I booked the Leeds event. A month later came another call: 'Wayne, are you free on Saturday, May 13th?' This time it was a booking in Pontefract. It was going to be a busy weekend, but Rotherham to Leeds to Pontefract was certainly doable.

The weekend in question came around and it was looking good: Thursday in Rotherham, Friday in Leeds, then Pontefract on the Saturday. Except that wasn't quite how it panned out. My phone's predictive text had entered Rotherham, when I'd intended to write … Rotterdam. Somehow I made all three of my appointments, but it was a rather more arduous few days than I'd anticipated. And it was one weekend when I definitely didn't have any spare time to relax in an airport lounge.

14.

FITNESS

If you're a man or woman of A Certain Age, take a moment to cast your mind back to Sunday afternoons in the 1980s, weekly instalments of *Bullseye*, and that show's most coveted prizes. I'm not talking about the tumble dryers and jetskis, but the items given away to contestants whether they were successful or not: a poseable foam recreation of the show's mascot, Bully.

Bully, a fat-bellied anthropomorphised bull, seemed to be the embodiment of darts back then, but ask yourself this: why did a bull make sense for this mascot? Well, yes, because a dartboard has a bullseye, but still: why not a magnificent gazelle, or a sleek and majestic stallion? More to the point, why was Bully always given away with an accompanying beer tankard?

Some might call it a caricature of the darting world, but it's hard to argue that beer and the bellies that went with it weren't at one point synonymous with darts. Don't forget, it's not so long ago that players in big championships would routinely place drinks orders from the stage while they played.

Back then, fitness wasn't even a big part of wider culture, particularly among men and definitely among darts players.

Diets, regular exercise and things like 'carbs' simply weren't talked about in darting circles: people were literally drinking and smoking on the oche, and from what I've been told by older players, if you'd mentioned the idea of fitness back in the seventies and early eighties you'd have been laughed out of the auditorium.

With its roots in the pub world, darts was almost seen as an *escape* from the responsibilities of sensible living. In those days it was also seen as a way of avoiding the demands for physical fitness imposed by more well-regarded sports, rather than how we see it now: as an activity that exists at a different point on the same sporting spectrum.

Slowly, however, things began to change. Rod Harrington, who came along in the late eighties, is a good example of someone who helped turn the tide: throughout the nineties and into the 2000s while he was scaling the heights and becoming a double World Matchplay champion he was always banging on about fitness.

This wasn't because he thought it made him better than anyone else, but because being in decent shape genuinely made him feel good. Steve Beaton, a former world champion and quite possibly the most liked person on the planet, was the same: I'd go so far as to say Steve was the closest darts came in that era to having a fully-fledged male model in its ranks – his nickname was Bronze Adonis, and he'd never be the one propping up a bar at 4am, or eating a large greasy kebab on the way back from a venue. He always looked after himself and even now, in his late fifties, he cuts an impressive figure. (In the past I've been accused on Twitter of 'gushing' about Steve – all true. What a man.)

Phil Taylor's another one. He was always on some sort of fitness regime. It was a different one each time you'd see him. He'd go on and on (and on) about the qualities of certain foods, forever searching for the right combination. You could be at breakfast during a multi-day tournament and you'd come back from the buffet with your plate piled perilously high with every fried item known to man, and you'd find Phil sitting there quite happily with a solitary banana. A few weeks later you'd find yourself tottering back from a different buffet table in a different hotel, with yet another teetering mound of breakfast, and you'd see Phil with two gallons of orange juice and two rashers of bacon. 'The last diet didn't agree with me,' he'd say, then two weeks later you'd see him again and he'd be on the muesli.

If the above sounds at all dismissive, it's not intended to be – Phil once lost about three stone in six weeks, and searching for a fitness regime that works for you is the most effective step in making sure that when you do find the right method, you actually stick to it. The players are now running their profession as a business, and even though there were professionals back in the seventies, eighties and nineties, they didn't approach their work as a streamlined operation. They didn't even care so much about getting sponsors – if they were approached, that was fine, but they didn't put much thought into their brand, or how they were perceived.

Fitness plays a huge role in both image and performance. You want to look the part, but you also need to be match fit. Players are working harder now than any darts professional from back in the day. And when they're not playing, they're travelling. You do need to be fit, to a certain point, which means you can't do what people did in the eighties and nineties: drink before a game, drink while playing, then go to the bar and drink some more, before doing the whole thing again the next day.

There's no such thing as time off for players these days. Well, not unless there's a global pandemic. I noticed during the first lockdown in The Cursed Year – the greatest and worst example of mass time off in living memory – how numerous players were saying that because they had nothing else to do they'd use their permitted exercise time to go out and run a 5k every single day. I can only imagine that if Bristow had done anything similar in the early eighties he would have been ridiculed, but I'm pleased to say darts players, and the community around them, are a little more savvy these days. These are players who understand that fitness is important. I believe the players of this era are schooling the players of the next, and I hope at some point in the future we'll end up with darts players and football players able to stand side by side, with no obvious difference between them.

In Gerwyn Price's case that's not far off, to be fair. He's a former professional rugby player, and having had the misfortune of bumping into him in the past I can tell you it's like making sudden contact with an antique sideboard. When I think of darts players of the 1980s, bumping into them might have been more like colliding with a bouncy castle. Price is like solid oak and nothing's going to move that guy.

But if you haven't seen your toes in a while, don't panic. Let's not pretend that in order to be a decent darts player you need to have a six pack, a bum as pert as a pair of satsumas and the ability to complete a daily triathlon before breakfast. We're standing in front of a board and throwing things, not running through Death Valley in the 135-mile Badwater Ultramarathon. (I think we can all agree that a normal marathon sounds bad enough, and whoever came up with the term 'ultramarathon' needs their head examining.) But I do believe that at the very least you need to be 'darts fit'.

Among other things, that means working on stamina. For a start, with all the travel involved you need the stamina of a long-distance walker if you're hoping to navigate most airport terminals without missing your flights. But it's on the oche that fitness matters most: it's vital that you're able to play at your best for periods of up to two hours at a time. Your game needs to be consistent, and you need to be able to summon that game at the right time, regardless of what you've been doing the day before. You can't be tired after a day of play. I'm not as heavy as I used to be, but while I'm not fit by any normal metric, the fact that I'm darts fit means I can stand in front of a dartboard and pummel away, knowing that I won't ache the next day.

If being tired from playing darts sounds unlikely, all I can say is you've never played proper darts. It really is a full-body endeavour.

How well you're able to compete will ultimately depend on your stance. Whether we're taking out the bins, making a cup of tea or throwing a dart, we all have physical manner-isms and little habits when we're doing certain activities. Some-times those habits don't really matter, but often they do, and getting things wrong can have dire consequences. Squeezing your teabag against the side of the mug to extract as much leafy goodness as possible isn't going to do any harm; removing the teabag and throwing it across the room at your partner is not a wise strategy. (I should add here that 'milk first' is the behaviour of a psychopath.) Likewise depositing your rubbish in clearly marked bins for general waste, recycling and composting has long-term benefits; tying a bin bag to the back of your car and driving round your neighbourhood until the streets are lined with a trail of household debris will eventually get you punched by a neighbour.

My point is that with darts there are some habits that'll become part of your long-term throwing style, while other habits can prevent you from playing darts long-term at all. In an ideal world we'd all just lift our arm, bend the elbow and hinge it there. But it's impossible to throw a dart accurately like that.

I do a lot of darts coaching, and with new players the forcing of the dart is often a problem, normally because they are trying to throw the dart from A to B as if it's a bullet. In doing that they're stressing their body and pushing themselves to an unsustainable limit. You want to propel the dart with enough controllable force that it travels as directly as you can make it, and if you're forcing the dart it won't be long before you end up experiencing pain, arthritis or trouble in the shoulder, your elbow, your back … The list of potential ailments goes on and on.

Footballers have trouble with their knees and groins; darts players generally have problems with their wrist, elbow or shoulder. Jelle Klaasen, the 2006 world champion, was one of the young bucks and a self-styled lean, mean, fighting machine: an impressive operator. But he's always had what I'll call an over-zealous wrist action, and during the Premier League a few years back he ended up having wrist surgery because the action he'd developed was just too much. So, early on, if you notice repeated throwing is causing strain, try a few different stances, and see which is most comfortable.

I appreciate this may not sound like the most complex or scientific approach, but don't be fooled by the simplicity. The key here is comfort. If you're hoping to become a professional, you could find yourself using this stance and throwing action hundreds of times an hour, several hours a day, day in, day out for the next few decades of your life. It really needs to stand the test of time, so know your body, *listen* to your body, and find a stance that's going to work for you moving forward.

And this is where overall body fitness comes in. You'll find a stance that works for you, but that's no use if your body won't let you keep that stance. I've known people change their stance midway through games because their legs, calves or insteps are hurting. But if they stand differently with the weight distributed strangely, that'll cause problems with their accuracy.

As many of you know, I've had my own battles with overall fitness over the years. I've gone from twenty stone to thirteen, back up to fifteen-and-a-bit, and I can tell you now how I feel mentally when I've put a bit of weight on or lost it. When it goes on, I lose concentration and I feel like my body aches. I feel like my legs are under constant pressure, as if they could buckle at any time. When I was bordering on twenty stone I was a lot younger, around thirty, so I could hack it, but even then I had trouble concentrating.

My biggest problem was always diet. For a long time I had something of a penchant for KFC or, as we called it back in the day when we all had more time on our hands, Kentucky Fried Chicken. To be honest I feel like 'penchant' is doing a lot of heavy lifting here. More accurately I'd describe my passion for the Colonel's secret blend of eleven herbs and spices as something bordering on an obsession.

I won't ever forget the time I got so carried away at the ordering stage that I ended up having to lie about who the food was for. The thing to note here is that Donna always requests the same items – three pieces of chicken with chips, that's it – but somehow I found myself at the counter ordering a fourteen-piece bargain bucket, a Family Feast containing six pieces of chicken and four portions of chips, plus a litre bottle of Coke.

It was only when the server asked me how many cups I'd need that I realised I was in serious danger of embarrassing myself. I was ashamed of what I was about to consume. Not so ashamed that I amended the order, of course, and bearing in mind I was the best part of twenty stone at that point he obviously knew I was going to smash pretty much all of it, but that's not the point. Panicking, I turned to the packed restaurant, looked 'over yonder' at an imaginary family member, bellowed: 'DO THE KIDS WANT A DRINK???' and pretended to hear my fictitious companion's response. I turned back to the server. 'Four cups please!'

It was only then that I noticed Donna, in a different part of the restaurant and having seen the entire sorry escapade, slowly shaking her head at me. We collected our food and made a hasty exit.

As a darts player, putting on weight (or losing it) can have unexpected impact on your game. Phil Taylor has yo-yo'd as much as I have over the decades, and what I've seen in his game is that when there's weight loss you can end up over-leaning when you throw – you feel like you've got more energy and as if you can get into positions you couldn't before. But you never want to over-lean on the oche. (That's a very common fault with darts players. 'The nearer the board the better, right?' they think. Well, no.)

When the time did come for me to address my own weight, it was hardly an overnight transformation. The first step came in 2006, when I was playing in the Premier League, and I decided to make a concerted effort to be fitter. I wanted to be at the peak of my powers, both mentally and physically, and began to accept that I was simply too heavy to be at my best. So I bought a rowing machine.

If you've ever bought a rowing machine, I'm pretty sure what happened next will come as no surprise. It gathered dust for a while; then we moved house and the machine got taken with us and placed in the conservatory, where it stayed unused until it was dismantled and put in the shed. When we moved again I didn't even take it to our new place, I just removed it from the old shed, dumped it in the skip on moving day and drove off. They say that where there's a will there's a way, but the problem back then was that I had the way, not the will.

The crunch point eventually came a few years later, when I stopped playing professional darts. Suddenly all the 'reasons' I'd once had for my diet and lifestyle went out of the window. For instance I could no longer blame being on the road all the time for those 'necessary' service station KFCs. I could no longer blame 'being sociable after an event' for excessive drinking. All my crutches had been taken away, and now I had to stand on my own two feet. No longer living out of a suitcase, I could have more control over my routine and my diet: I ate more healthily, I exercised a little more. Eventually I became leaner and, as a consequence, felt much fitter. As the weight continued to fall off I had more energy, and with that I found I could concentrate more: I had mental energy as well.

And mental energy is all too rarely discussed. In the darts world mental fitness feels like it's on a twenty-year delay compared with physical fitness. In the nineties and 2000s players started to get their bodies in shape, and it's only in recent years that they've made a real effort to address getting their minds in shape too. In fact, the topic of psychology in darts is such a big one that I feel it deserves its own chapter. Spoiler alert: that's what's coming next.

15.

MIND GAMES

I t's perhaps no surprise that Wayne William Mardle, being a proud Essex resident, should have made a living through darts. Archaeologists rummaging around, as is their wont, in Clacton-on-Sea back in 1911 unearthed a sharpened wooden spear, which remains one of the oldest ever pieces of evidence that Neanderthals in the area were chucking sharp objects around, over 400,000 years ago. They called it the Clacton Spear – coincidentally the name of Essex's third best Britney impersonator.

These days most of us find that the expression of our hunter-gathering instinct is limited to poking around to see who's offering free delivery on Just Eat, but I do believe throwing things at other things is deep within all of us, meaning that we're predisposed towards darts. If you're wondering why javelin throwing isn't therefore bigger than it is, that's another conversation for another day, by which I mean I haven't really thought my theory through, but the point is we all have a built-in ability to aim and throw. Some better than others, of course, but we've all got it.

Thing is, when you're competing on a stage in front of thousands of people, darker forces come into play. It becomes more than just a question of instinct or hours spent practising. It turns into a mind game.

Winning in darts is actually the simple bit when it comes to being a professional. The hard part is the losing, or the feeling as if you might. Only when you're on the back foot do you find out what you're made of, and whether you're up to the task. And the thing with being on the back foot is that it only takes one more wobble for you to be on your arse.

American philosopher and basketball player Troy Bolton once noted, during a battle with his own mind, that the answer was simple: 'I've got to get my head in the game.' How right he was. Focus is necessary for any sportsperson, and over the years I've seen darts players try all manner of innovative, daring and sometimes foolish solutions. I've seen the lot, investigated by players suffering from varying degrees of desperation: meditation tapes, yoga, coaches, sports psychologists, hypnosis ... If it involves having a chat or lighting a scented candle, a darts player's given it a go.

And who can blame them? These are players who've hit a tricky spot in their career, and have sought out someone (that 'one person') who can help them turn it all around. I'm a great believer in the power of advice, and in both the offering and accepting of tips; I often coach players at my darts school, and it's easy to see the improvement in their game after just an hour or two at the bottom of my garden. But I'm not someone who thinks another person can change my innate thought process. 'You'll be under pressure; when that happens, think of a meadow' – wouldn't work for me. At the risk of sounding controversial, when I want to hit a treble 20, I'll think about hitting a treble 20.

Of course if it works for you, even if it only works for you because you *think* it works for you, fill your boots. But one thing I do find interesting in relation to sports psychologists is that in absolutely every case I've come across, those supposedly brilliant experts – and let's just say these people aren't exactly offering their services for minimum wage – have been dropped by players. The conversation generally runs like this:

Player: 'I went to a sports psychologist and it worked!'

Me: 'So you're still with them?'

Player: 'No.'

Me: 'Why not? Your game's regressed again.'

And the reason players don't go back, even when their game is slipping back into old habits, is that in their heart of hearts they know the sports psychologist didn't really do anything the first time: in most cases any 'fix' or sense that it worked was down to the placebo effect. Any subsequent slip in performance calls into question the effectiveness of the whole thing, and then there's no point in going back. Unless something works at the most intense time, when you really *need* it to work, you're just not going to stay with it.

If you do find yourself struggling with confidence ahead of a game, don't forget that sometimes it's all about how you frame a situation. A few years back there was a quote from Michael van Gerwen before a game, when he was talking about taking on Phil Taylor. 'He's the greatest of all time,' Van Gerwen said, 'but I'm the best of all time.' At first glance that might make very little sense, and the more you think about it the more it might sound like absolute nonsense, but to my mind Van Gerwen was making a very important distinction. Phil's record of wins will never, ever be touched. You could print it out and hang it in the Louvre. Maybe down the back of the Louvre. But still the Louvre. That record of wins? The mark of a great player. But when you look at MvG, you see someone with an *ability* that hasn't been matched. In other words, he's the best.

Pressure always made me nervous, which is pretty standard, but when I was nervous I'd find that my hand used to go cold and my legs would go weak, which was less standard and not at all helpful when I was standing and throwing. These days in moments of high pressure my hands and legs go even colder and even weaker, but I'm not playing professionally now so those moments are few and far between.

Back in the day I found the best method of dealing with that situation was to try and charge right through. I conquered the problem through sheer speed – 'Just do it, don't think about it.' Sometimes I'd rush, but that was my way of coping. Sometimes the darts went in, sometimes they didn't.

Later on I'd also find that if I was feeling apprehensive, I could calm myself down by arriving at a venue as much as four hours before I was due on stage. Some players would find themselves getting even more wound up by being in this situation for so long ahead of their game, but for me it had the opposite effect. The first hour was spent sitting around doing very little – making sure everything was in place, getting tickets sorted for the family and so on – and then I'd just immerse myself in the situation, as frenzied and hectic as it might have been backstage, until it felt normal. As soon as it felt normal, I could relax. Not a technique that would work for everyone, but it certainly did the trick for me.

Once you're on the oche, the whole situation can change again, and you'll likely be confronted by a player doing anything they can to put you off. Sometimes that means physical interference. One reason big games have a different coloured carpet – the exclusion zone – around the throwing area, signifying an area into which an opponent cannot step when someone's throwing, is that during one notorious World Matchplay event in 2002 between Keith Deller and Rod Harrington, each was apparently so intent on derailing the other's game that they ended up inadvertently kicking each other and hovering around each other in close proximity. On both sides it was seemingly an attempt to skew the throwing, and if so, it worked. After that the 'exclusion zone' was put in place.

But more common – and far less easily detected by officials – is the verbal and psychological damage players will try to inflict on their opponents. All players have mumbled under our breaths at times. I was a talker. Mainly to myself: 'Come on, Wayne, come on.' Other players found this off-putting. Barney, for instance, told me to shut up. As did Phil.

What you're really trying to do, if you want to psych out an opponent, is ruin their rhythm. Darts is one of those games where you're throwing every few seconds, and if you get thrown off, the whole rest of your game can go down the toilet.

I used to have a method of throwing people off where I invited them to notice I was doing something – a small mannerism for instance – and once I knew they'd seen me do it, I'd wait for them to expect me to do it again. But then I *wouldn't* do it. That used to drive people mad: it was mental torture. Of course, once they'd settled into the idea that I wouldn't do it again, I'd do it randomly. One instance of that is that when I hit a 180, I'd collect my darts and start to walk back; by the time the other player had lifted their arm up ready to throw I'd be just over their shoulder, and I'd raise my own arm up to salute the crowd. My opponent would see this out of the corner of their eye. So sometimes I'd hit a 180 and I'd see them hesitate, waiting for me to do my salute before they got ready for their shot. Except, as I say, I wouldn't always do it. And then it worked even better: they've put themselves off their own rhythm, and I've not even done anything. I'll just be walking back calmly, as if butter wouldn't melt.

One thing worth remembering: mind games are usually indulged in by players who know they're not as good as their opponent.

Sometimes problems are nothing to do with other players, or even their own expectations. Sometimes problems just appear out of the ether, and to any darts player there's one phrase that inspires fear like no other. It's more terrifying, even, than the phrase 'unexpected letter from HMRC'. And it's just one word: *dartitis*.

If that sounds like a made-up word, that's because it is, although (a) as Thor notes in *Infinity War*, all words are made up; it's not as if they grow in the ground like potatoes just waiting around to one day be chanced upon by humans, (b) dartitis existed long before it had a name, a bit like ghosting and Milton Keynes, and (c) regardless of how you feel about the etymological validity of its name, the existence of the affliction itself is not open to debate.

Dartitis manifests itself in the most destructive way a darts player can experience: it stops them throwing the dart. As you can imagine, unless someone else is going to bring the dartboard itself closer to your dart at high speed, not being able to throw your dart is something of an impediment when you're standing on the oche.

The best description I've ever heard of dartitis came from Eric Bristow, who succinctly described it as 'the fear of missing'. And if anyone was in a position to know, it was Eric himself. Eric was the first player in whom I saw dartitis. I was still a kid, so this was long before I knew what it was called, but there was no mistaking what I saw that day in 1987 at the Unipart British Championship: my hero, and the best young player of his generation, simply not able to let his dart go. I remember thinking: 'What on earth is this?'

Afterwards I could hear the commentators explaining that it was a condition where a player panics and can't release the dart. Then I heard Eric talking about it, and it started to make more sense. I've played matches before where you have to throw, it's your turn, and you're so nervous you'd really rather not. Dartitis is more than feeling nervous before an important throw, and it's more than simply feeling the pressure of a big event. It's the thought – the *knowledge* – that if the dart were to leave your hand, it would miss the target.

The result? It stays in your hand. It feels as if the dart isn't just resting in your hand, but superglued to your fingers. You can be in the spotlight on a stage in front of five thousand people, the tension so clear to hundreds of thousands more at home, and in your mind there's just one thought: 'There is no way I can release this dart.'

Dartitis is a word players don't like to hear when they're playing. Just like how in golf the players don't like to say the word 'shank', and actors will only refer to *Macbeth* as 'the Scottish play'. Darts players are the most straight-talking bunch you'll ever come across, but if you see that something dodgy might be happening in someone's game you'll beat around the bush like an Australian egg-whisking fanatic. 'You alright? Letting go alright? Feeling alright? How's your action?' Literally anything but the d-word. They know what you're getting at, you know they know what you're getting at, they know you know they know what you're getting at, but because you haven't said the word it's possible to have a straightforward conversation about it.

I did have an opportunity to speak with Bristow about it once. He had his darts with him, and he held one up. 'See this?' he asked. 'I've got this dart in my hand. I could let it go right now and throw it anywhere. Put a dartboard in front of me, and it all falls apart.'

It's a horrendous thing to strike a player, and I remember it happened to a young lad called Berry van Peer when he was playing against Gary Anderson at the 2017 Grand Slam. It was harrowing to watch – there were people in the crowd with tears in their eyes because they knew what turmoil Berry was going through. Imagine not being able to play the game you love, because you simply can't let go of the dart.

There have been plenty of studies on dartitis over the years. Some players have recognised their own issues in the findings;

others have said all the research has been irrelevant. The strange thing about dartitis is that because it's not related to any outside factors like stress or performance, it can appear at any time, for no obvious reason. It descends on players who've been fine for decades, and it descends on twelve-year-olds who've been throwing for a month. But just as curious is that for some lucky players it can simply stop, as suddenly and as inexplicably as it began. There really is no rhyme or reason.

For Eric, it never got better. Sure, he could still take part in a darts tournament for fun or as part of an event, but it was always under the black cloud of dartitis. The effortlessness for which he'd once been so well known just didn't exist any more, and he never got over it. It dominated every throw for thirty years. I truly believe it killed his love for the sport, and it's not hard to see why that would be the case: he played through it to his dying day. And I mean that literally. He was doing a corporate event at the Echo Arena on the day he died, and he was throwing with dartitis even then. He still loved darts, but I'm not sure he enjoyed playing it.

While I'm lucky enough never to have experienced dartitis, it's worth remembering that dartitis is totally arbitrary and bears no relation to any particular player's mental or psychological strength, or lack of it. I've heard people say things like: 'Oh, I'm too mentally strong to ever get dartitis.' Some people really do think it's a weakness, and they reckon it's irrational to fear the completion of a very simple task – to hold something, then to let it go.

If only it *was* that simple. Eric Bristow was the most mentally robust human being a lot of us ever met, and I don't think there was ever any doubt about Eric's self-confidence or self-belief. He had the lot, and still it happened to him. If there's any good to be found in what happened to Eric, it's that in the eyes of many his condition destigmatised dartitis: his affliction showed that it really could happen to anyone, and that it would be unfair to make judgements about those who did find themselves in its grip.

I do understand how the fear of missing can take hold of someone's mind. But I also believe that missing, weirdly, is simply part of the game, just like a glass can't be half full without also being half empty. You can't have a game of darts where every shot goes exactly where it's supposed to. Imagine if that did happen, and how boring every game would be.

You're not going to get every shot you go for. I've seen it so many times – someone throws a dart, it comes out of their hand strangely and it misses the board entirely, or they walk to the board with dart still in hand. Is that the onset of dartitis? No, it's just being a darts player. These are the things *every* darts player experiences. If you've played darts I can guarantee certain things have happened to you: you've missed the target; you've had a bounce-out; the dart has unexpectedly gone in an odd direction. Play often enough for long enough and you'll do everything. I've brought the dart back, it's come out of my hand and it's flown backwards over my shoulder. What happened there? Absolutely no idea – and I was a professional darts player at that point. Even today, Gerwyn Price, the world champion, is dropping his darts all the time.

Do you want to know the biggest secret in the world of darts? Look at the world's best players over the generations – Eric, then

Phil Taylor, now Michael van Gerwen – and they've all got one thing in common. They miss more often than they hit.

This might seem improbable to an outsider. How, they might ask, is it possible to be one of the world's best at something, while still being capable of missing shots? After all, you could understand a footballer failing to score from time to time, when every striking situation is slightly different and there are eleven grown adults getting in their way. Even with penalties there's a goalie flapping their arms around. But darts is a totally controlled situation, right?

Well, to an extent, but that's never entirely true. However much a player might have a chosen stance, we won't stand the same every time, we won't feel the same every time, and we won't use the same power every time. Those who've come closest to being robots are Eric, Phil and Michael, but like I say, even they miss – and they miss a lot.

I watched some events recently and thought that even I could have reached the final, and I'd not thrown a competitive dart for a decade. The winners' secret? They just happened to be better than their opponent that day. This is really blowing the lid off the whole thing, but it's true: to win PDC ranking events, you needn't always be brilliant. You simply need to be good enough, often enough. If you're a struggling player and those words don't help you get your head back in the game, you really are beyond saving.

16.

RIVALRY

Björn Borg versus John McEnroe. Blur versus Oasis. WH Smith versus John Menzies. History is littered with intense and bitter rivalries, but sometimes the passion at the very heart of such rivalries can create something rather beautiful.

In the 1800s, for instance, inventors Nikola Tesla and Thomas Edison were each protective of their electrical innovations: alternating current and direct current respectively. (The internet's great, isn't it?) But they were also so critical of each other's work that the energy from their feud quite literally sparked the invention of heavy metal, and with it the band AC/DC, who have now been rocking out for over 150 years.

Similarly, rivalry in darts has given the world some great entertainment over the years, one recent example being the ongoing bunfight between Gerwyn Price and Gary Anderson. There's no two ways about it: those two chaps have an extremely strong dislike for each other, can't stand each other's personalities, have no intention of kissing and making up, and are not bothered about who knows. If one of them were to punch the other during a live televised final it wouldn't surprise me – there's already been proper, physical shoving during games between those two, which is foolhardy at best on Gary's part considering Gerwyn is a former professional rugby player and still has the physique of a brick shithouse with adjoining shed.

Like most rivalries it's all incredibly silly when you take a step back, but Gerwyn's not the kind of guy to back down from a feud. Even at the best of times he's very much an aggressive darts player. He's loud, he screams at opponents, and over the years the DRA have fined him accordingly. I imagine his lifetime bill with the DRA well exceeds £20,000 at this point, all of which basically boils down to aggression on the oche. He's an antagoniser and he annoys opponents, but he seems to feed off that adrenaline rush in order to play well: he's a two-time and back-to-back Grand Slam champion and now the world champion, having beaten Gary 7–3 in a very one-sided final at Ally Pally in January 2021.

My first experience of a darting ding-dong was when I played youth darts. I quickly learned that in youth darts there's a strong hierarchy based on age – the difference between a twelve-year-old and a fourteen-year-old can be immense in terms of size, ability and intellect. And while I remember being friends with a lot of players who were older than me, I also remember deciding that just because they were older than me that didn't mean I couldn't beat them. In fact, it was important to me to beat those older players. But rivalries intensified when we moved on to playing league darts.

There were rivalries between teams – we couldn't let certain teams beat ours – but there were also rivalries within teams. At the heart of that is the fact that you want to be the best player in the team, or at least good enough to make sure you don't get left out the following week. You want to be as good as you can be, and that means being better than the rest. And so I found myself in a strange situation, which I can absolutely guarantee has happened to more players than would like to admit it, where I was wishing ill on a team member. I'm not proud of this, but I'd find myself hoping that while our team might win against another, there'd also be a player on my own team who'd have an absolute stinker so that I'd stand more chance of keeping my own place. Is this me being an arse, or is it normal?

I'll give you a specific example. I can still picture the scene: I was in my teens and struggling at the time to keep my place in the Essex team. One of our most improved players was a guy called Alan Ware and I had a feeling his skill – *his skill specifically* – was going to be the reason I was kicked out of the Essex county team. He was an absolute certainty to be selected. We were meeting at a pub called The Plough in Romford, on Gallows Corner, and we got a call: it looked like Alan might have to work late, and chances were he wouldn't make it. This sounded absolutely ideal to me: he couldn't be selected for the following weekend if he wasn't there.

'We'll give him another ten minutes,' the organisers said.

'No, come on, let's go,' I yelled.

Looking back now I'm a little embarrassed, but at the time that was the way I felt, and it summed up how desperate I was to be in the team. My outburst didn't go unnoticed. You know those moments when you say something in the pub and everyone suddenly goes quiet? If this had been a movie, a pool ball would have teetered on the edge of a pocket, the jukebox would have suddenly stopped playing and the pub dog would have whipped its head round.

As it was, George Harris, my mate in the team and one of my best friends to this day, just turned to me and went: 'I know what you're playing at here.' Alan turned up and played the darts of his life, totally oblivious to the curse I'd attempted to place on him. I, meanwhile, was playing abysmally. He was so nonchalant: for him, all roads were leading to playing for Essex, taking my place in the process. 'If I get picked I get picked,' was his take on playing for the county. 'I don't care and I'll probably have to work that day anyway.' I was a disgrace on the night. I'm a team player, or so I like to think, but I wished him every defeat. And eventually he did lose. Even thinking about it now I know it was wrong. It's not that I'd wanted to do better – I'd wanted someone else to do worse.

So I learned an important lesson that day: wishing ill on a rival doesn't make you feel any better, even if you win. And I'm telling you all this now because I really hope you pull yourself back from a similar reaction if you find yourself in a similar position – or, if you're already wishing ill on rivals, you accept it's a horrible thought process.

I'm disappointed, in a way, that I never went on to develop a proper arch-enemy – a Moriarty to my Holmes, a Pringle to my Dorito – because I've always quite fancied the idea of having a nemesis, mainly for purposes relating to drama, spectacle and general attention seeking. Petty rivalries, though? Oh, I've experienced one or two of those. Back in the day there was definitely beef between Peter Manley and me.

He and I would play each other a lot back in the day and he was a classic 'putter offer' – he'd play within the rules but it would feel like he'd bend them, just a little, in his favour. He wouldn't kick or push you, but he'd be pleased if you were thrown off your game. He was the type of person I referred to in the previous chapter and he was known in darting circles as A Talker. There's a famous incident between Manley and Adrian Lewis that you can still see on YouTube, where Peter's literally talking to Adrian as he's throwing. It's not the done thing in my view, it's not right, and it's not professional. He's now the chairman of the PDPA, but back then it was a shame if Peter felt the need to do all that, because he was a fantastic darts player and a former world number one, who really didn't need to stoop to anything.

But Peter could be desperate to win games. And while we were friends – we'd go on holidays together (always Vegas), our wives would shop together, and we could be thick as thieves – when we played each other there was real rivalry.

We'd be having breakfast together and he would be so cordial on the surface. 'Playing today?' 'Off to the venue later?' 'Best of luck!' But this chit-chat was like the polite-looking tip of an iceberg whose more bastard-like submerged lower portion was on a mission to smash the hull of a New York-bound passenger liner. I'd watch him waving his sausage around over breakfast, giving me all this encouraging chatter, and I knew what he was really thinking: 'I've got to win.' As a result, I found that sometimes I'd try *too* hard against Peter – unnaturally hard, in fact. Did it make me a better player? Absolutely not. It made me worse. I couldn't relax. There were times when he beat me as a result, but to be fair (to me) there were times when I beat him too. That rivalry has never subsided, even now when I'm out of the professional game. When you compete against him once, you compete against him for life. And he knows my feelings about his chairmanship of the PDPA ...

Other intense rivalries can be just as complex. Take the situation between Phil Taylor and Raymond van Barneveld. I know they respect each other incredibly highly, but their rivalry is so fierce that they'll berate each other on a regular basis in front of anyone who'll listen.

Even though they'd been playing against each other in opens and challenge matches for years, the true rivalry started in 2006, when Raymond joined the PDC. There was a huge amount of hype around his move from the BDO, and Phil, who'd been the king of the PDC until then, wasn't prepared to take this new competition lying down. The general mood in darts circles at the time was: 'Phil is better than Barney.' We knew Phil was pretty much unbeatable at the time. So it'd be up to Raymond to prove he was the best, which quickly turned out to be a bit like asking a dog to prove it could lick its own doodah.

When Raymond did indeed make good on his promise (to beat Phil, not lick his own doodah) the rivalry really picked up some pace. Over the years I've been lucky enough to compete alongside each of them, share meals with them and take planes with them, and there's always been a certain *frisson*. They'll eat together, have fun, wake up and have breakfast together. Then they'll play against each other that night for fun ... But it's not fun. Not quite. They'd each rather lose to *anyone* else. Their rivalry has run so deep and for so long that it's part of each of them now, and they'll forever be rivals: the Babybel and Dairylea of the darts world.

There are plenty more examples of rivalry: Michael van Gerwen has experienced it with both Phil Taylor and Adrian Lewis. Then there's John Lowe versus pretty much anyone who was too much of a show-off. As I mentioned earlier in the book, John took a dim view of flamboyance and didn't mind who knew it, which ruffled a lot of feathers back in the day.

As time went by fans started to take sides: for every darts fan who liked Eric for being brash or Bobby for being a showman, there were plenty who respected the quieter, more refined approach of John, a man who tucked his shirt in, cared about his collars and didn't smoke on stage. He even commanded respect, a little grudgingly, from players who couldn't otherwise stand him.

There's one classic darting rivalry that wasn't quite what it seemed. Jocky Wilson's rivalry with Bristow was based on little more than one being from Scotland and the other being from England – as I mentioned in the Legends chapter, they didn't actually hate each other at all. The hype over the years was anything but fact: they got on and they liked each other, and for all his faults Eric was a loyal friend until the day Jocky died.

Getting involved in rivalries is the easy bit. Settling them? A more tricky manoeuvre. You'd think it would all come down to winning a competition. But despite being grown men (many of whom are in fact still growing, but that's middle age for you) you'll find that for most darts players success or failure is a lot more complicated than looking at a scoreboard and admitting defeat. Success or failure is often measured well away from the oche. I remember Bristow gloating once to Bobby George about winning five world titles.

'Five world titles,' Bristow goaded, 'and what have you got?'

Bobby, of course, lived in a seventeen-bedroom mansion at this point, and had no insecurities at all about his talents as a player, so he calmly reminded Bristow of all this, adding: 'Imagine how much bigger my house would be if I *did* win five titles.'

Eric wasn't exactly living in a wheelie bin at the time, but with his retort Bobby had conjured that rarest of darting miracles: a virtually speechless Eric Bristow.

These days you'll find darts players subtly flexing their egos via an array of four-wheeled contraptions: someone turns up in a Porsche, another player wants a Maserati, then the next week someone'll turn up in a £100k Audi or a top-of-the-range Range Rover. At the time of writing, Michael van Gerwen has recently purchased a Bentley. Ostentatious? Not for me to say, dear reader. Not for me to say. What you'll generally find in darts is that rivalries tend to stay relatively polite. It's like the situation with Tesco and Sainsbury's: they're in competition, but they can co-exist peacefully on the same high street without the Saino's crew sneaking out at dead of night and fire-bombing the nearest Tesco Metro.

The reason for this, I believe, is that because darts players are mostly working alongside each other at close quarters, competing against each other every other weekend (or, in 2021, what seems like every other day), staying in the same hotels and practising on the same boards, there's really no space for anyone to act up, or be truly disrespectful to another player. Falling out is easy when you're not seeing someone ten times a month, but when you're living in each other's pockets it's in your best interests to find the good in everyone. There's not really one big darts player I'd avoid purely because I couldn't stand them. Even taking Peter Manley into account. (Only jesting, 'One Dart'.)

True, some have been rather more difficult than others to get along with, and there've been a few players who on occasion have been out of order and may have deserved their comeuppance, but like I say Bristow was the nearest anyone would get to being hated and he'd almost always counter that by pulling something surprising and kind out of the hat. He was so respected that most people let the five-time champ get away with everything.

'Bonhomie' is a word thrown around with too much abandon these days, but my theory is that at the very heart of the darting world's good nature is the fact that while we might compete against each other, nothing any of us does can actually have a material impact on anyone else's ability to get a good score.

In curling some messer is always trying to bang your stones out of the way; in football there's invariably a fool jumping around in front of the goal trying to make your life harder than it needs to be; and boxing would be significantly more straightforward if some fella wasn't trying to deck you. In each of those sports someone else doing well always means you'll do less well, and vice versa. But in darts nobody's trying to tackle you on your way to the oche, or whack a tennis ball at your head when you're collecting your darts.

So, for all my talk of rivalries big and small, there's very little to worry about if you're planning to get into the sport. Your success or failure is always on you, and you alone. In fact, something I realised rather late on in my professional career is something I wish I'd known right from the start: there may be other players trying to do better than you, but at the end of the day the biggest rivalry you'll ever encounter is rivalry with yourself.

17.

BOOZE

B ack in the day my dad used to drink with the football legend Jimmy Greaves before Greavsie went on for Tottenham. As in, actually *right* beforehand. They'd get through a couple of halves together in the Corner Pin round the corner from the ground, then my dad would wish Jimmy a good game and send him on his way.

After the game Jimmy would invariably reappear for more drinks, before making his way home. Now it's worth noting that during this period Greavsie was literally an alcoholic, which takes the shine off things slightly, but my point is: imagine the scandal if that were to happen now. Imagine Harry Kane neck- ing lager in the Corner Pin half an hour before kick-off!

A bit more of the shine's taken off this scenario by the fact that the Corner Pin shut in 2010, and in fairness I'd quite like to see a Premiership match in which all twenty-two players are staggering around, off their heads on booze, but the point I'm attempting to make is that in most sports turning up and doing your job after a couple of drinks would be, shall we say, rather frowned upon. You can't exactly picture Mo Farah warming up for the 10k by going on a pub crawl, or Tom Daley steadying his nerves by snorting tequila before attempting to pull off backwards somersaults with two-and-a-half twists during a ten-metre, 40mph plummet. The only thing he'd be able to guarantee is the plummet.

When it comes to darts, it's more complicated. Darts is a sport that started life in pubs, meaning that booze and darts go hand in hand like a pint glass in … well, a hand. But the days of players on the telly at a major championship, with a pint in one hand and a fag in the other? Those are long gone.

For a while now I've been saying to the PDC and anyone who'll listen that they have to totally do away with the drinking culture in darts, and you'll be surprised by some of the push-back I've heard from other players. Their defence is usually weak, to say the least. The most ridiculous argument I've heard is this: 'The audience is allowed to drink, so why can't we?' Well, for exactly the same reason you don't see Novak Djokovic tucking into strawberries and cream during the final of the men's singles, or Harry Kane eating a pie while waiting for a ball to nod into the back of the net.

While you won't see it being conspicuously consumed on Sky Sports, I think most dartists have played after a drink or two. You might think the danger is that you'll do badly, but in a way there's also danger in doing quite well when you're half cut. You begin to feel like it could actually be the *reason* for your above-average playing when in reality it's more like accident, coincidence, fluke, or all three at once. If you have a drink, play well and it somehow works out fine, you need to remember that no, booze isn't necessarily what made you play well – it just so happens that you had some booze and you played well *on that occasion.*

Grow too convinced of the notion that three pints and a Bacardi Breezer represents some sort of darts-improving elixir and you'll soon run into problems when you start to rely on alcohol, particularly if you get to the stage where you're playing three hundred days a year. You won't have a long career, you could do your body some serious damage, and you might drink yourself to an early grave. Particularly when the darting prowess falls by the wayside (reason: you were drunk the entire time) and all that's left is the alcohol. Failure's hard to process at the best of times; coping with failure when you're also an alcoholic is unlikely to end well. Even with players who view alcohol as a social thing, rather than some sort of crutch they've convinced themselves they need to do well in tournaments, I've seen plenty of underachievers because of it. It's brutal.

An exception to this rule is Monky (Colin Monk), who could consistently put it away and still storm to victory. Colin was a brilliant player who should probably have got to world number one and done a lot more, and I'm sure he wouldn't mind me saying that he could be absolutely paralytic and still play championship-winning darts. To this day I still don't understand it. It caught up with him of course, because once age came into the equation he couldn't hack the pace of it any more, but in his younger days he'd be absolutely steaming by the time he got to the oche.

I've seen Colin more or less unable to lift his head, then two hours later battling it out in the final of ranked events. At tournaments you'd see Colin at various points in the day as he gradually descended into drunkenness, and each time you'd wish him luck in the next game, assuming this would be the one where he'd go out. An hour or so later, you'd see him again.

'Did you get through, Col?'

'I did, mate, yeah.'

Interestingly enough, since packing in darts Colin's a lot more health conscious. And he can still play darts to a decent level – quite incredible really, and I do admire him a lot.

Nowadays I can look at players in the darting environment drinking too much and I can shake my head. Not at them, but at my younger self. I feel embarrassed now about staying up and getting blotto before a major final. I think: 'I could have done it differently.' Would the results have been different? Who knows.

These days players are a bit more savvy: in 2021 your average new darting professional is more lean, more focused, more immersed in the game than his or her predecessors. Part of this is down to the fact that there's more prize money, so the stakes are higher – as recently as the early 2000s a big win at darts wouldn't necessarily be life changing, while these days there's everything to play for. But it's also down to darts players wanting longer careers, and simply wanting to live longer. Bear all that in mind and you can see how the old plan of 'I'll just get pissed and see what happens' doesn't fit in with the modern mindset.

How this impacts the game as a whole remains to be seen. I've long insisted that if we cut the booze completely, massive blue-chip conglomerates would get involved in the sport, putting more money into the game and individual sponsorships. We'd see better TV interviews before and after games too, because players would be thinking more like a professional and less like someone at a thirty-person stag do in a brewery.

But, again, I'm not going to pretend I haven't enjoyed the odd drink or two over the years. In my early twenties I flew to Germany with some other lads – back then darts was what drew us all together, and if you went on a run and made a couple of quid that was great, but in reality we mostly just wanted to hang out together.

The first mistake that weekend, I later realised, was to meet early at the airport. If you're anything like me you know that once you're through the scanners you're in a strange, timeless zone where money and sobriety cease to have any real meaning, a bit like Vegas with more branches of Dixons. Inevitably we got on the pints, and I've never been a big pint drinker because I find the sheer volume of liquid hard to tolerate, meaning that just as inevitably I was in a complete state by the time I boarded the plane. Things went downhill from there: a morning's drinking blurred into an afternoon's drinking, which then became an entire day's drinking.

The next morning my mate and darts partner Mark Landers knocked on my hotel room door so we could share a cab to the venue together, but there was no reply so he set off by himself, figuring I'd made my own way there. I was still in the room, comatose. I eventually woke up later that afternoon, having missed the entire event.

'How did you get on?' Donna asked when she called me that day.

'Not very well,' I said.

'Oh well', she replied.

I didn't have the heart to tell her what had actually happened, and as news from the tournament filtered back to me the full horror of the situation started to take shape. It was very unprofessional behaviour; mind you, at that point I wasn't yet a professional. I was simply a young man enjoying himself. So, I told myself, that was alright.

My rules on specific beverages have always been quite strict. Vodka and cranberry is generally my go-to, though I've found that asking for cranberry in mainland Europe results in blank expressions at the bar and the sort of confusion you'd expect if you asked for them to serve your drink in a bird bath. As a fallback I'm happy to accept gin and tonic, vodka and tonic, or a nice dry white wine, whereas nothing with a Coca-Cola mixer shall pass my lips because it will make me retch within minutes. Come December I only need to hear 'Holidays are coming' and I'm calling for Huey. I *will* accept an umbrella in my drink, but I draw the line at sparklers.

I take a firm line on hotel minibars too: they're a rip-off, although the 'will I/won't I' question vis-à-vis Toblerones and £10 miniature Bacardis is largely academic considering how frequently I've checked into a hotel and been told at reception that they're really very sorry, sir, rooms with minibars aren't available. I can only assume the reputation of darts players precedes us.

For one weekend, and one weekend only, cocktails became a big thing for me as well. The weekend in question was during the Desert Classic in 2005, when I was playing at Vegas's MGM Grand; the draw was the night before and they put on a nice little dinner for everyone who was playing. Well, that 'nice little dinner' saw me coming face to face with my first ever mojito, and I have to say I found this exciting new potation both refreshing and strangely moreish.

After about a dozen I headed out into the casino and while I do remember throwing hundred-dollar chips onto a roulette table, the subsequent details of the evening are less clear. The next afternoon I awoke in a sea of hundred dollar bills. I worked out that I'd somehow accumulated about $8,000 more than I'd gone out with. How I won it, I'll never know. Did I even win it? I could have robbed a bank. I'd had a total blackout. Since then, mojitos have been saved for (a) Vegas when I (b) have no responsibility whatsoever and (c) can trust myself to stop at three.

In any case, I found a way to bring a bit of Vegas spectacle to even the most dilapidated UK conference centre. At the height of my game, a height that on reflection might have been considerably higher if I hadn't spent a significant proportion of the time off my face, I decided that as I didn't enjoy the crap beer that came out of the taps at darts events, I'd start bringing my own drink. The result being that for a good few years I decided champagne was the way to go. I'd turn up with my own bottle of Laurent-Perrier or Moët and, rather shamefully, my own champagne flute, and I'd make a big show of popping the cork.

'Why are you drinking that?' people would ask.

'Because I can,' I'd say.

'Because you're a twat,' they'd think. (And Kevin Painter would actually *say* it – rightly so, in hindsight.)

It was just for effect. I didn't even particularly like the flavour, although I eventually got a taste for it. I forced myself.

It was a tough job but someone had to do it. Thing is, I've always had showmanship in me. And you could argue that my usual routine of chucking on a Hawaiian shirt and dancing around on stage was enough of a show in itself, but I felt like the champagne was the cherry on the cake. In the cold and rather sober light of day I can now muse on the very fine line between showman and dickhead. I really didn't like the beer they served, though.

There does come a point when every darts player is forced to confront his or her intake and for me that point came in Vegas – where else? – during the summer of 2004. I'd reached the final of the PDC's third Las Vegas Desert Classic, a huge event at the Vegas MGM Grand.

Remember when Tyson fought Holyfield in 1997? Same place. Some aspects of my own experience at the MGM were similar – for instance, the huge LED screens above the stage, which had once flashed with the rotating names MIKE TYSON and EVANDER HOLYFIELD, were still there, and were now reading PHIL TAYLOR and WAYNE MARDLE. (It's quite something seeing your name up in lights like that, and it's hard not to feel empowered. I remember seeing the stage and thinking: 'Right, I'm going to maul him. I'm going to absolutely maul him.') Unfortunately that's where the similarities end, mainly because while Tyson famously left the ring having torn something off, namely a not insignificant portion of Holyfield's right ear, I staggered onto the stage after tying one on.

By that I mean I was pissed. I wasn't paralytic, but equally I hadn't been to bed for two nights. I was competing against the world's best player, in a major final, live on Sky Sports, and I hadn't slept for forty-eight hours because I'd been knocking back champagne, vodka and mojitos, and gambling like a fiend.

The game was due to start at midday, but I'd taken up residence at one of the hotel bars at 6am. I remember when I'd first arrived at this little bar in the middle of the casino – a bar no bigger than ten feet wide, with a little opening for the barman and a handful of poker consoles on top – I'd said to the barman: 'Are you open?'

And he'd gone: 'We're always open.'

It was music to my ears. By that point I'd already been drinking for so long that I'd convinced myself I was sobering up, even though of course I wasn't sobering up at all and was, in fact, becoming progressively more drunk. The reality of the situation was not something that troubled me when I ordered a vodka and cranberry. Then another. Then several more.

I was having a great time as the clock ticked closer and closer to midday. Somewhere in the blur of it all Sharapova won the Wimbledon final, beating Serena Williams, and I'd had a bet on that outcome so I was jumping around the place like a lunatic. And of course by this point the darts fans were all wandering in, and I was there in my Hawaiian shirt so even in Vegas I wasn't exactly blending in, meaning that the fans were all coming over for photos and autographs.

The barman was watching all this happen – and bear in mind I'd been there two or three hours by that point, and he'd been serving me for the duration, so there was no doubt about it: I was drunk. The barman went: 'I have to ask, who are you?'

I said: 'Well, there's darts on, isn't there?'

'Yeah,' he nodded. 'I know that.' And then this look of absolute horror crossed his face. 'Hold on,' he went. 'Are you playing?'

'Yep, I'm in the final.'

He looked me up and down, paused a moment and replied: 'Can I bet on the other guy?'

'Yes, you can!' I declared triumphantly and, with that, I staggered off to face my fate. I turned back, and he was just kind of staring at me, with the most subtle shake of his head. You know the head-shake: the type you'd usually only get from a disapproving parent. And at that point I remember thinking: 'Wayne, there's a very slight possibility you might have overdone it.'

This came into focus (and for me, it was pretty much the only thing in focus) when I got downstairs to the practice room and found Phil, already practising. Safe to say, Phil hadn't exactly been on the piss during his time in Vegas, and the only refreshment he had in front of him was a small portion of fruit. He looked me up and down and said: 'What the FUCK has happened to you?'

'Nothing,' I said, attempting to gloss over the fact that I probably looked like I'd just been dragged away from a brawl outside a tiki bar. 'I'm fine. I'm fine!' (If someone tells you they're fine once, they might be – if they feel the need to tell you twice, they're not fine at all and are almost certainly pissed.)

I asked Phil what he'd been up to in Sin City and he told me matter-of-factly that he hadn't left his hotel room in the last seven days. 'I'm here to play, and win, then go home,' he said, adding that in his entire time there he'd only left his room to eat and play darts.

I looked at him standing there, all ready to lift another trophy, and I said: 'Phil, I think you might win this.'

Which, of course, is exactly what happened, although strangely he only beat me 6–4 in sets (and I actually won more legs than him), and it was a pretty close game considering I was off my face on Vegas! As for my trusty barman, who'd been such a friend when he was pouring out those vodka and cranberries, and such a stern parent when I'd staggered off to meet my defeat ... Well, despite his claim that he was always open, I didn't see him again the next day, or the day after that. I like to think he did go and place that bet on Phil winning; that he pocketed the cash and jacked in his job on the spot. At least one of us would have been lucky that day.

I'd like to leave you with a teachable moment here but the following year I played Phil again, in another final, I did the whole game totally sober and he beat me 6–1. So I'm buggered if I know. Logic suggests there's probably a sweet spot somewhere between total sobriety and staggering up to the oche shitfaced after a two-day bender, but if that sweet spot exists I've yet to find it.

18.

THE MEDIA

W hile some darts players are Chatty Kathys, it's no secret that others seem to have severe difficulty talking and standing up at the same time, and you may not be surprised to hear that I've lost track of how many times I've told darts players they should have media training. As a sport we're not as bad as footballers (*nobody's* as bad as footballers) but on occasion we're not far off, and I've been campaigning for new players to get schooling in how to behave on camera since at least 2005. I convinced the PDC to set up a session once, and no bugger turned up.

My motivation wasn't entirely selfless. When I was still a pro there was a period when TV crews figured out that most players were either monosyllabic, totally incomprehensible, likely to accidentally swear or all three, so if they wanted to speak to a player at a tournament they'd always pick one of two people: me, or Phil Taylor. If Phil said no they'd ask me, and if I said no they'd ask him. It would go round and round in circles.

And that's what led me to eventually say: 'Look, Phil and I can't be doing all the heavy lifting here, other players need media training – they can be on TV week in, week out, and at the moment they're making a mockery of the game.'

The players I'd suggested for media training were not happy with this idea. 'We're not doing it,' they huffed. 'We're there to play darts, not speak, we don't want to do media training and we're not changing our minds.'

Many of those players are still knocking around, and I'm dismayed but not surprised to report that they still have trouble stringing together a coherent sentence once the camera's on them. All I can say is that it's only through having been dependable on camera that I showed the TV networks I could be a capable commentator and pundit, and without having shown them that I'd have had a rather challenging retirement, workwise. I still think those stubborn players should embrace the opportunity to show the sports world how articulate they can be, because when retirement comes along they'll be grateful for whatever options they've got. As well as helping players seem interesting, which in turn will build their brands, media training would also help newer players avoid making absolute fools of themselves.

And I know a little about that. If I can offer up-and-coming darts players one piece of advice, it's this: for the love of Christ, if you're doing an interview ask in advance *what's actually happening*.

In 2006 I was in Holland for an international event and at the time I'd been experiencing a slight drop in form. Three weeks earlier I'd been beaten in the World Championship semis, yet again. By Phil Taylor, yet again. I'd begun the year thinking 2006 was going to be my year, but it really was not, and the gradual realisation that I was going through a barren period was affecting my performance in Holland, too. To be frank, I didn't really want to play at all, but it was too late to back out, so there I was. There were four of us – Peter Manley, Mervyn King, Phil Taylor and myself, in theory England's four best players – taking on four Dutchmen, but when it was my turn to play Co Stompé, I messed it up. And I knew that because I'd done *that*, my next game would be against Raymond van Barneveld, and I had to win to progress.

So losing to Co was a big blow. I'd gone into it thinking I'd be able to beat Co, and I'd messed that up, so I knew that with the way I was feeling I had little chance against a player of Barney's calibre. This all dawned on me just as I was coming off stage following my defeat against Co, at which point I was accosted by a film crew: 'Wayne, will you do an interview for SBS?' SBS was the main Dutch TV channel, so I agreed – after all, it's not unusual to do a quick post-game chat, so amid the noise and the hullabaloo of the major darting event we sat down and had a relaxed chat about the game, just to pass time before we got the signal that the interview had started and we were going out live.

'Wayne, what happened?' the host asked, making smalltalk.

'I'm pissed off!' I replied. I really wasn't in the mood to be doing an interview, let alone making smalltalk beforehand. 'Fuck's sake!' I continued. 'I don't like losing! I'm fucked off ... I'm playing shit.'

The host asked me a few more things about the game, which weren't exactly getting me in the mood for the interview. 'These,' I pointed out, 'are the questions you should be asking when we're live.'

'We're live now,' he replied.

'We're not live,' I said. (It's amazing how many thoughts it's possible to have in the space of a split second, but the main one I had at this point was: 'There is no way we're live.')

'We are,' he confirmed, 'and there you are on television.'

He pointed across to a TV monitor tuned to SBS, proving that we were, indeed, currently broadcasting across Holland, also confirming that I'd just let rip with a string of expletives on live television. If you've never seen the expression of a man who looks like every bodily organ is suddenly about to fall out of his arse, I recommend you search this video out on YouTube. My face is an absolute picture.

In my defence, not once did the host say, 'Sorry about that, viewers.' Not once did he pull me up. Not once did he say, 'Wayne, just mind your language a little, please.' But there was no point making accusations about whose fault it was. Particularly as I was resigned to the fact that the blame lay squarely at the feet of one W. Mardle. The damage was done. I got back into the green room to a slow handclap from the other players and every-one else who'd seen the broadcast, and I looked over to Donna, who was sitting quietly in the corner. When it comes to body language there are certain things one can do to soften the impact of precisely how bad a calamity appears, and Donna's pose that day – head in hands, gently rocking – is not one of them.

'Was it that bad?' I asked.

She took her head out of her hands, looked me full on and said: 'That was horrendous.'

Not that it makes any difference to the excruciating appear-ance I made that day on Dutch TV, but my defence will always be that I should have been told we were going live, as soon as I sat down. And it's certainly true that while darts players often don't help a situation, a car-crash interview can be just as much the fault of the interviewer.

Sometimes I wonder if presenters need a bit more training themselves. Ahead of games, players still hear questions like my absolute least favourite: 'Do you think you can win this?' Now I've mentioned it, you'll probably start to notice just how frequently it's asked of players, and as a former professional myself I can tell you there's really no sensible way of responding, which is why most players tend to reply with something sarcastic or flippant. What do they expect someone to say? 'Probably not, might just get the bus home now'?

The media never tire of asking you which of two players you'd like to play, when everyone knows that whatever you say the real answer is always 'the worse of the the two'. Then there's the helpful habit of reminding you of all your recent failures just before you go on in an important game, and perhaps throwing in some compliments about your opponent's recent form too, just to twist the knife a little more. I still laugh when I think of the time Roland Scholten was interviewed just before going on to play against Phil Taylor, and the journalist opening with 'So, Roland, you've played Phil Taylor twenty-four times and lost twenty-four times' – shortly before he lost to Phil for the twenty-fifth time.

I first came across this strange interview technique when I was just sixteen, playing in the 1989 British Youth Championship on the BBC. Tony Gubba decided to interview me, and I'd never been on TV before but I was in the final against Andy Mallett, so I ended up in front of the camera. Tony's first question: 'Are you any good?' What an opener! I looked at him and thought, 'You what?' I didn't know what else to say, and eventually I responded with: 'Of course I am, I'm in the final.' I looked at him like he was an absolute imbecile. What a ridiculous question!

Perhaps I should have gone easier on Gubba that day – as an interviewer I've had my own fair share of sticky moments and they're not ideal when you're on live TV. At the 2015 World Championship I was interviewing Phil Taylor and by that point, well, he wasn't the Phil Taylor the darts world once knew. He'd changed by then. He was no longer the best player on the planet. Imagine being the best at something for two decades, then waking up one morning and realising you're on the slide ... It'd be a shock to the system, and Phil hadn't taken favourably to the situation.

Rather than work through it, he was taking a lot of that frustration out on other people in the darts world. He became aggressive in games, and in interviews he became even more argumentative than usual. Maybe I should have been treading more softly, but I asked him: 'You played really well in spells, but you allowed Kevin Painter to get to you, why was that?'

'Why are you asking me that?' he scowled. 'You're putting me in the shit.'

He was getting very defensive and really quite irate. But I'm not one to back away from that type of situation, so I doubled down: 'I only asked you a question about why you were mentally strong against the others and not Kevin.'

'YOU'RE PUTTING ME IN THE SHIT, WAYNE.'

We left it there. I was glad we were live on TV because I picked up a strong sense that in any other scenario he might have punched me. Imagine me and Phil rolling around a TV studio trying to hit each other. Ridiculous.

Even on a good day Phil ended up becoming unpredictable in those last few years before retirement – he used to pop up on TV and say, for instance, 'Am I allowed to say bollocks?' And like I say, he was once one of the more responsible players, which just about sums up why we don't interview certain people. I often get fans asking: 'Why didn't you interview James Wade or Mark Walsh?' I'm not going to say it's because we're afraid of their answers but the fact is 90 per cent of the time they're just trying to be awkward. It does them no favours and it's car-crash TV.

I do think darts as an industry has a responsibility to present itself in a good light. While I can't say that fiasco in Holland had a massively positive effect on the sport's reputation, elsewhere I've been conscious of wanting to put across a better image for the sport. The main reason is that I'm old enough to remember the period when darts was widely ridiculed. There wasn't as much money in the game back in the day, and money always makes people take things more seriously.

Now players are aiming to win £500k rather than £20k, darts is 'important', but back before darts was officially recognised as a sport the media saw it as an easy target for cheap laughs. One typical example came in a sketch by the comedians Mel Smith and Griff Rhys Jones in the late eighties, in which darts players Guy 'Fatbelly' Gutbucket and Tommy 'Evenfatterbelly' Belcher battled it out in a drinking contest.

Some might argue that was a slightly questionable caricature of a working-class sport from two privately educated

Oxford graduates but that would be grossly unfair, because one of them actually went to Cambridge.

Either way, that sketch pretty much summed up the public's attitude towards darts. I'm not going to pretend certain players didn't fuel that perception – naming no names there were plenty for whom a name like Guy 'Fatbelly' Gutbucket was less a caricature and more an understatement – but the more that perception solidified, the more the media looked to support it with negative stories. It became a vicious circle. You'd see Phil Taylor scoops, details of players not paying their tax, and then 'Here's a photo of Bristow drunk in a kebab shop' or 'Oh look, Chris Mason's been arrested again'. It was the way they wanted to portray the sport, and when there was a big event on where there'd be something positive and worth celebrating, they'd hardly report on it.

A classic example of the negativity came in 2004 when Andy Fordham became world number one and was billed as 'the 30-stone world champion'. The facts, I suppose, weren't up for debate: Andy was indeed world champion and there was nobody arguing he couldn't have stood to lose a couple of pounds. But why bring his weight into it?

Darts always seemed like it lacked glamour in the eyes of the media. Pool got *The Hustler* with Paul Newman and *The Color of Money* with, well, Paul Newman again. Darts has never had its moment on the big screen. On the small screen, however, darts had a secret weapon – a way of crowbarring itself into fifteen million homes every weekend for fourteen years via the primetime, poseable rubber bullock-strewn weekly darting quiz show extravaganza *Bullseye*.

Bullseye was shown on ITV and hosted by the sadly late but indisputably great Jim Bowen. Both the show and its host are still incredibly fondly remembered by darts fans of a certain age, and it's testament to *Bullseye*'s genius that it's remembered just as fondly by the darts professionals who'd frequently turn up on the show to win prizes for the contestants.

In the days before fame was as easy as doing something unspeakable with a wine bottle in the *Big Brother* garden, being on television was a big deal, particularly as there were only three or four channels on offer for most of *Bullseye*'s time on air. I know it's a prospect so shocking that it would probably hospitalise kids brought up on countless algorithmically driven entertainment options tailored to every obscure whim, but back then if you wanted to watch TV you had to make do with what was on. And I don't think that's necessarily a bad thing: if you only watch stuff you know you already like, you never find out anything new. And I know for a fact that over the years *Bullseye* being 'what happened to be on' converted hundreds of thousands of ITV viewers into people who were passionate about darts.

One of the things for which *Bullseye* is most fondly remembered is its really rather startling array of prizes. These days you'll tune into ITV and find Ant & Dec giving away a four-bedroomed house; back in the eighties it was more about what to put *in* a house: a set of coffee tables, a power drill or a washing machine, and maybe a hammock for the garden. That said, the world of darts can be a rather small one and I personally know people who went on the show and picked up caravans and trips to Jamaica.

Not to be sneezed at, and it's worth remembering that while the less glamorous prizes might not exactly set pulses racing in 2021, back in the day a top of the range (or even middle of the range) microwave oven was a luxury to some of the people who went on the show. Loads of these people were exactly like the guys I'd be playing darts with when I started out: between work and with a family to support, or just about making ends meet with low-paying jobs. I personally know someone who came off *Bullseye* with £250 in cash, and uttered: 'That's great – for me, it's two weeks' money.'

The genius of Jim Bowen is that he displayed an almost superhuman degree of empathy and warmth with everyone on *Bullseye*, from darts pros who'd missed a key shot to contestants who were down on their luck. You'll still hear stories from people who were on the show: Jim would hang out with them all day, he really did want them to win a bit of cash and a prize or two, and he'd be genuinely gutted if they didn't. As for those notorious speedboats, presented to confused winners who lived a four-hour drive from the nearest bit of coastline? Well, they didn't have to sit rotting on bricks on a Loughborough driveway: a little secret of the *Bullseye* world is that whatever Bully's star prize happened to be, the show would basically buy it back off you if you didn't want it, effectively giving you the cash equivalent instead.

After nearly a decade and a half on air, *Bullseye* came to an end in 1995 but did return to screens a few years back, with the comedian Dave Spikey taking Jim Bowen's role but hardly filling the master's shoes. I'm no TV critic and the closest thing I have to a media studies degree is a subscription to *TV Times*, but my assessment of the *Bullseye* reboot is that it was load of old shite. Where Bowen found a way to balance warmth and good humour with a solemn reverence when it came to the actual darts element, Spikey seemed to take the mickey out of everything and everyone, and then for no discernible reason you'd get Fizz off *Coronation Street* coming out to throw for charity.

No disrespect to Jennie McAlpine, who's carried that role with considerable aplomb in a period covering two decades and multiple daring haircuts, but where was Phil Taylor?

More to the point, you might be thinking, where was notable-at-the-time darting funnyman Wayne Mardle? Well, I considered the whole endeavour so offensive that I think I might be the first professional in darts history to have actually turned down an invitation to go on *Bullseye*. Back in the nineties I would have paid money to be on there, but I was not prepared to go on that show when it was a farce with Spikey. In my opinion they should have let the show die, and if any execs are reading this and wondering about another reboot I say this: *Bullseye* should stay off air until technology and budgets allow a convincing Jim Bowen hologram to take the show back under his virtual wing.

And one thing I believe should stay off air for all eternity, regardless of how far technology advances, is that clip of me on Dutch TV. Sadly I don't have much say in the matter. It still goes viral again from time to time, a decade and a half after it first aired, and in Holland my humiliation has become an annual event: it's become such a sensation that SBS wheel it out once a year on a compilation of classic televisual bloopers. I suppose, at the very least, it's nice to have a legacy.

19.

VEGAS

If you were to ask me to name one place on the planet that's totally like you see in the movies, that comes exactly as advertised, where dreams are made and broken, where you're thrust into a full-scale multi-sensory overload from the moment you set foot there to the moment you leave, I'd have one answer: Stockton-on-Tees. But if you pushed me for a second, it'd have to be Vegas.

No word of an exaggeration: Vegas is the best place I've been on earth, which considering I've never been into space also means it's the best place I've been in the entire galaxy. In The Cursed Year, YouGov surveyed Britons and asked them whether they'd visit the moon if guaranteed safe return and nearly half said no, with top reasons ranging from 'not interested' and 'no point' to my particular favourite, 'nothing/not enough to see or do'. To which I say: fair enough. If you offered me a seat on the first commercial trip to the Sea of Tranquillity or yet another visit to Vegas, I'd take Sin City every time.

I simply cannot think of anywhere I'd rather be, which is lucky considering darts has extremely strong ties to Vegas, with big events like the US Darts Masters, the Las Vegas Open, the PDC World Series and the Desert Classic having required regular trips to the neon jungle over the years.

I made my first visit back in 2000 – I'd wanted to go to Vegas for years and it was, indeed, darts that got me there. I'd seen that there was going to be a darts tournament held at the Riviera Hotel so I said to George Reeves, my friend and my sponsor at the time: 'The North American Open is being held in Vegas and I think I can do some damage.' It was a PDC event and I was a BDO player at the time, but in a feat of generosity that still makes very little sense to me George agreed to pay for my flight (and Donna's) plus hotels, and I was off.

I'd been used to playing in conference centres and convention rooms back in the UK, and it was only when I stepped into the Riviera's own convention room for the Open that I realised just how different this particular tournament would be. We've all got an idea of the sort of convention room these things are generally held in – pokey, functional boxes with beige walls, covered in carpets whose gaudy patterning was unwise when they were fitted thirty years ago and nothing short of a psychedelic nightmare in the present day. The sort of rooms in which reality-show contestants belted out Josh Groban ballads before the shows started spending money on the auditions. Rooms that have seen a thousand corporate away days, and will see a thousand more before anyone considers sprucing up the decor. Well, Vegas was something else. It was borderline *opulent*, at least compared with the rooms I'd experienced back in the UK, and pokey it was not: Donna and I reckoned it must have been the size of four football pitches.

And when we walked in, standing about two football pitches away, were the great and the good of the darts world: Phil Taylor, Eric Bristow, Dennis Priestley, John Lowe. The superstars were all there, and back at that point I'd met each of them briefly, but not to the extent where I felt like any of them exactly knew who I was. In fact the one I'd met most often was Bristow, who strolled over while I was sitting with my friend Jill.

His opening words: 'Who the fuck are you?'

I could tell from the look in Eric's eye that this was hardly cheery banter, and it was going far beyond the usual BDO vs PDC tomfoolery. Eric always wanted to get in your head – he was often a bully to me, frankly, in those early years, and while our relationship would change and strengthen over the years there was no way I could have known that back then. Also, bear in mind that when I'd previously met him I'd been through the whole 'you don't know me yet, but you will' routine with him, and had met him a few times subsequently, so he definitely knew who I was. I could have recoiled at that point, but instead my response was simple: 'You know who the fuck I am – piss off.'

You could have cut the air with a knife. Eric and I had found ourselves at the centre of a circle of bystanders who were all waiting for it to kick off. Instead, he proposed a wager. 'I bet you a thousand dollars,' he scoffed, 'that I win more money than you this week.'

Well, back then I didn't have a spare thousand dollars knocking around, particularly a spare thousand dollars to throw away in a bet. But Bristow wasn't exactly at the top of his game at that point, and I thought to myself: 'I'll win more than he will.' So I told him he had a bet and that for safe keeping he should give his thousand dollars to Jill, who could adjudicate.

'Don't worry about that,' he went. 'I'll win anyway.'

By this point my adrenaline was really pumping – he'd been a childhood hero of mine and all I could think was: 'You absolute arse. You pig of a human being.'

To cut a long story medium-length, the draw for the main singles was done and, wouldn't you know it, I ended up playing Eric. As it turned out, I ended up playing *well* against Eric. 'Good darts, Wayne,' Donna said encouragingly after each leg. But by the final leg, when Eric knew he was done, he'd started taking the piss out of Donna, and behaving like what I can only describe as a massive man baby. It was 2000 and I was already gaining the persona of being jovial and a bit of a clown, but when he had a go at Donna the red mist descended and after I told him never, ever to mock my missus, he saw the change in me and realised he'd pushed my buttons too far.

And then I beat him.

What I then said to Eric isn't something I'm proud of. Perhaps I shouldn't have said it. But he'd pushed me so hard. Mock me, fine – but don't try to intimidate my soon-to-be-wife. I just had to let him know I had no respect for him. I hit the winning double, walked over to him, and said: 'Remember. You're finished. Now go away.'

For once, he was lost for words. And from that moment our relationship changed. The next day I found myself sitting round the pool in the Riviera, drinking beers with Donna and Peter and Chrissy Manley, who we didn't really know but they made us feel so welcome, and would go on to become close friends. But we were also drinking with ... Eric and his wife Jane. I remember thinking: 'This is the life of a professional darts player that I want.'

I also remember realising how the old cliché about bullies had been proven true: stand up to them, and they crumble. I later found out that Eric's done that a million and one times to new players – sometimes people are bullied into submission, but I wasn't going to be one of them. I wouldn't say Bristow did me a favour back there in Vegas, because quite frankly the whole debacle was horrible, but I'm pleased I stood my ground. I'm also pleased I had the ability to pull it off – if he'd beaten me in that game, who knows what might have happened? I might never have taken up darts professionally.

And did I get that thousand dollars? Did I buggery, although I did take the opportunity to bring it up once or twice (translation: one or two dozen times) over the years. Years later he'd pretend not to remember any of it, but I'd always say: 'I would have taken that grand had you not welched on your bet, but I got a lot more value than a thousand dollars out of you.'

So that was my first experience of Vegas, but it hardly put me off. In fact I've been back every year since, sometimes multiple times in a year. Normally if you tell people you've been to the same holiday destination twenty-six times they'll ask you if you're bored of it, but to that I say: there are shows and restaurants I've been meaning to go to in those twenty-six years and I still haven't got round to them. I'll never get bored of that place.

My first piece of advice when it comes to Vegas is that when you're visiting, you need a plan. Many a holiday has been destroyed by blokes indulging in over-zealous planning, and

I can assure you I'm not usually one to whip out PowerPoint presentations around the pool, but when it comes to Las Vegas you really need to go in with an idea of what the coming days will hold. There's absolutely no point in saying you'll have a nice stroll to whichever hotel you fancy – you can walk aimlessly for six hours and all you're doing is tiring yourself out. So make plans, head for somewhere specific, and don't get distracted.

Second, do your homework about where you want to stay. Most hotels will accommodate you, but some are further away from everything than you expect them to be.

Third, and this is most important, you need to budget. You need to be prepared for the fact that Vegas is built to make you put aside your normal responsibilities in life. Again, a holiday shouldn't normally be an opportunity to dazzle your other half with an Excel spreadsheet, but you seriously need to go in knowing how much money you've got, and how much (or how little) you're expecting to come out with. There have been many times when I've got a few days in and thought to myself: 'This is one expensive holiday.'

You do have to look after your pennies, because they absolutely will not look after themselves. This is the side of Vegas you'll see at 5am on the Strip: holidaymakers who've gambled everything, and lost. For a glimpse of what happens when people fall on hard times all you need to do is go to one of the pawn shops to the north of the Strip; you'll find the biggest array of Rolex watches you'll see in your entire life. Each one of them was once on the wrist of someone who came to Vegas and lost everything, but just needed one more fix. I like to think that of those hundreds of Rolexes there are a few former owners who've taken the cash back to the Strip and got lucky but, well, the fact that the watches are still in the pawn shop tells its own story.

And I've certainly had my own minor financial disasters in Vegas. One time I found myself playing poker for higher stakes than I was comfortable with; I'd usually change up about $1,000, but after a successful run I'd found myself in the position where I'd invested $6,000 into a pot.

This was way beyond my comfort zone but I was firm with myself: I'd play one more hand, see how it went, then walk away. You're probably wondering, at this moment, just how many men and women have come face to face with calamity by employing the 'one more hand' rationale, but there in the moment I just wasn't thinking straight. I'd decided the $6,000 – my original $1k, plus the $5k I'd won that night – was all mine. And it would have been if I'd cashed out, but I didn't, and I lost the lot on one hand, on the turn of a card. I stood up to leave. More specifically: I tried to stand up to leave. I realised my legs had stopped working. I couldn't get up. What with the panic and the anxiety, followed by the crushing defeat, my body just wasn't prepared for it. In fact, not only had my legs gone, but I was feeling rather queasy. Total strangers were asking if I was okay. Eventually I got to my feet, but my back had spasmed so badly through the stress that I couldn't walk straight. I couldn't even speak. Eventually I got to a pharmacy and found some muscle relaxant. They advised me to have a massage or a jacuzzi. I had both. And when I woke up the next morning I had to tell Donna I'd pissed all that cash up the wall. Being dealt with aces isn't always a good thing, I learned. Know when to fold, and all that …

Drama isn't only reserved for the high stakes games, either. I remember getting into a massive argument with some guy who'd got so drunk at the poker table that even though he'd announced 'All in', he ended up trying to squirrel away a bit of cash when he inevitably lost the lot. The pot was $2k and he was only keeping back $27, but that wasn't the point. If you announce 'All in', it's *all* in, not 'most in, minus your cab fare home and a bit extra in case you fancy breakfast', which is the defence this chancer was attempting to put forward. I demanded security be called. The clown tried to get up, but security stopped him.

'We've reached an impasse', the security guard shrugged.

'Call the police', I said.

I'll be honest, by this point I'd had a couple of vodka cranberries. It was getting a bit hairy. The dealer wasn't helping and just wanted rid of both of us. After an hour of this nonsense the police did actually turn up and that guy eventually gave me the cash, but as he walked off past me he made a gun with his fingers and put it to my temple, adding: 'You haven't heard the last of me.'

This wouldn't normally have concerned me too much – after all, Vegas is a big place, and how's this fella ever going to find me again? People sometimes say to me, 'Oh, you were in Vegas the same time as my mate Bob, did you bump into him?', which is a bit like saying, 'You're from the UK, have you ever met David Beckham?' Which I have, actually, which wrecks my point somewhat, but you catch my drift. Point is, it's easy to lose yourself in Vegas; some might even argue that's the entire point of the place. It's less easy to lose yourself, sadly, when Vegas also happens to be regularly strewn with posters showing your stupid grinning face accompanied by the words WAYNE MARDLE, along with details of precisely when and where you're due to appear. Not ideal when you're attempting to avoid a revenge killing. I thought: 'I need to leave town.'

Which I did, the following day. I mean, I was due to leave that day anyway, but still. I seldom argue around a poker table these days.

A rather less stressful trip occurred in the summer of 2002. In fact that's when I had my biggest Vegas win of all: getting married to Donna. We had the ceremony at the Flamingo Hotel Chapel, which may sound cheesy and corny and to that I say: yes, absolutely, quite frankly it was both and I wouldn't have changed a thing. We all wore Hawaiian shirts, it was brilliant fun and compared with the high-stakes military operation you expect from most weddings it came with absolutely zero stress.

I remember twenty minutes before the ceremony we were sat around the pool drinking margaritas and mojitos. 'We're getting married in twenty minutes, we should probably go and get changed,' I said.

'Suppose we should,' Donna smiled.

The sheer scale of Vegas is best explained by the fact that we'd booked our champagne buffet at Caesar's Palace, over the road from the Flamingo, and it took forty minutes to get there. 'Over the road' in Vegas means something quite different to 'over the road' anywhere else on the planet: up and down bridges, six lanes of traffic, a lengthy walk, not to mention ten minutes to actually get into a casino once you've supposedly arrived on its premises. It's almost as if they don't want you on the street, isn't it? Almost as if they want you to stay in the hotels. Almost as if they want you underground, spending your money.

That trip also sticks in my memory because it's one of the few trips to Vegas, and possibly the only wedding in history apart from [REDACTED FOR LEGAL REASONS] where the groom's come out of the whole thing with $27,000 more than he went in with. The whole visit was absolutely incredible: on my very first night I'd hit a jackpot for $5,000 on a Triple Flaming 7s machine at the Flamingo, which blared out a rendition of that 'We're in the Money' song as it paid out, and my luck continued in that vein for the duration of the visit.

On our second-to-last day there I walked past a $500-a-spin machine in Caesar's and tried my luck, which ended up netting me $2k. My hotel-room safe was full of twenties, fifties, hundreds ... When you see money piled up like that it feels somehow not real, which may explain why on the very last day I gave my niece and nephew $1,000 each and told them to go out and buy whatever they liked. My niece went into Gucci and bought a $500 handbag. On reflection my niece was perhaps too young to be spending half a monkey on a handbag – she used it to keep her crayons in.

The most ridiculous thing about my time on that $500-a-spin machine is that the Caesar's security guard came over to me and offered a limo to wherever I was going next. When I explained I was leaving Vegas the next day with my friends and family, he organised an airport drive in a sixteen-seat Hummer, which was like an island on wheels and still ranks as the most preposterous motorised vehicle I've ever seen. I asked why he was being so generous, and he suggested, very nicely, that perhaps I'd consider staying at Caesar's on my next visit.

I've had no further accommodation-related dealings with Caesar's in my entire life – these days I stay at Treasure Island, where I get a free suite, meaning they effectively pay me to stay there. It says a lot about Vegas that casinos can randomly offer potential future guests expensive limos, simply on the off-chance that someone might one day remember the favour and stay at their establishment, but knowing they probably won't, and still coin it in. Of course, it's not the casinos who are paying for this – it's you, or someone like you.

Another part of Vegas's appeal is the live shows, but you need to be careful when you're choosing which ones to go to. Tickets are never exactly what you'd call bargain priced – you can easily find yourself splurging hundreds of dollars on entry, and while we've established that something about Vegas convinces you dollars aren't Proper Money, there's no mistaking the priciness of a Vegas show if you grew up, like me, thinking of gig tickets as being five quid with a packet of crisps thrown in.

Don't get me wrong: some shows are absolutely worth the price. Lionel Richie, for instance, is a stupendous showman who totally understands how to entertain an audience, but I have to say the most amazing show I've ever seen in Vegas was by nineties R&B boyband Boyz II Men, best known for songs like sultry bonkballad 'I'll Make Love to You', and their global smash 'End of the Road'.

The latter is a song I consider to be total genius in a market-ing sense, on account of the fact that it can't help but reso-nate with listeners: most of us have lived on roads of some sort during our lifetimes, and nearly all of those roads will have had an end. Usually two ends, in fact – if it's a road with only one end you're more likely to be discussing something like a cul-de-sac and I really don't think the global pop audience of the 1990s was ready for a double-hyphened song title.

Anyway, the entertainment value of that band was absolutely outstanding. It was in a small auditorium at the Mirage with about six hundred people in the audience, or 603 if you include the members of the band who'd frequently walk off the stage and into the stalls, chatting with their fans.

There were times when a Boy II Man would be mingling with the crowd and I felt there really wasn't much difference between those velvety-voiced ballad purveyors and the times when I'd reached down myself to high-five fans at the Circus Tavern, the key difference of course being that I was exuding raw sexual magnetism and Boyz II Men, well, let's just say those lads could have learned a lot from me in my prime. But the point is, their performance was so respectful of the audience's presence.

At one point someone came out with hundreds of red roses and started giving them out to every woman they could see, and you bet I was jumping up and down to get one of those flowers. I eventually managed to get one tossed my way, but it was intercepted in mid-flight by a lady in the row in front of me, which left me absolutely fuming. I'm still fuming today although, actually, now I think of it, I suppose there's a very small possibility the rose was intended for the lady in front of me all along. And now, with you as my witness, I must confront the legitimacy of this grudge I've held onto for so many years.

But I'm certain of one thing: I really wanted that rose back in the day, and I still want it now.

Other Vegas shows are memorable for all the wrong reasons. There are two shows that stick in my mind for being, in different ways, absolutely disgusting. The first was Mariah Carey who, fair play, may well have a five-octave vocal range, but she forgot the lyrics to two songs and covered it up by singing 'la la la'. I'm sure you'll agree that being a performer myself I have a lot in common with Mariah Carey and I know there are better ways to cover up when you've lost the thread. Option one: hold the mic out and invite the audience to sing along. Option two: prance and preen a bit. Option 27,041: sing 'la la la' and hope for the best.

She also had seven costume changes in the space of ninety minutes, but the king of the timewasters is the man responsible for my other least favourite Vegas performance: Rod Stewart. It's not often I use the word egregious but I'm thrilled to chuck it in here because in my view Roderick absolutely took the piss that night.

I knew we were in trouble when he started the show by announcing: 'My daughter will be singing with her friend later on – that will be a treat for you.' No it won't, Rod, I've paid $170 per ticket to see you, not your offspring and her mate. They sang four songs which took the best part of a quarter of an hour although, ironically, the actual best part of that fifteen minutes was when they cleared off.

Rod had some more tricks up his sleeve. The first of which was to announce that he was going to try out some new material that he was thinking of playing at Hyde Park later that year.

He wanted to know what we thought of it. Well, I couldn't help myself. Once I'd finished booing I said to Donna: 'I'm out of here. This is taking the piss. He's got fifty years of material!' At which point Rod goes off stage, comes back on in a Celtic shirt and spends ten minutes kicking footballs into the audience! Kick out five, mate, don't kick out fifty. That show was an absolute disgrace and I can only assume the knighthood he later received was awarded for services to sheep farming because he absolutely fleeced us that night.

As well as those I've mentioned I've also seen shows by Celine Dion, Gwen Stefani, J.Lo and Britney – some of the biggest world's biggest divas, if you don't count Phil Taylor. (Phil, if you're reading this, I am of course only kidding.) But while there's a million and one shows you can see in Vegas, the biggest show is the Strip itself, the stretch of South Las Vegas Boulevard offering everything from water fountains and gondolas to exploding volcanoes and a reproduction of the Eiffel Tower.

They're all there to seduce you into staying on the Strip and, frankly, I don't take much persuading. It's well known that it's hard to find a clock in a Vegas casino but as far as I'm concerned they needn't have those measures in place – I've spent morning, noon and night gambling, playing darts and drinking in Vegas. Not because I don't know what time it is, but because I don't *care* what time it is.

In Vegas I'm detached from normal life and normal responsibilities. Nothing is real in Vegas. It's as if the real world has ceased to exist. And sometimes that's a rather comforting feeling.

20.

RETIREMENT

In 2009 I was ill with mumps and didn't throw a dart for six months. The year was a write-off; so 2010, I decided, was going to be different. It was going to be my comeback year. 'I'm going to hit the ground running,' I told myself, 'and I'm going to see what damage I can do.'

The damage, I'd discover, had already been done.

At my peak I'd been a fighter. Yes, I was a clown, but I also had an aggression about my game. I wanted to win. I'd fight it out. I'd *grind* it out. I always felt I had a game that could win. But in 2010 I discovered that game had gone. I knew it. Just as importantly, other people knew it. It was pretty evident I didn't have the fight any more. I just wasn't a threat, and I was turning into 'the decent draw'. I was the one people wanted to play. Not for the challenge, but because they knew they'd beat me. I wasn't feared.

There's a saying: whether you think you're going to win, or you think you're going to lose, you'll be right. I went from thinking I could win every game to thinking I'd fail. And I was right. I felt like I had nothing to offer. On the day of a big game there would be just one thought in my head: 'I'd rather stay at home and not get beaten.'

Crunch time came at one particular moment in 2010. I was due to fly to Canada to compete and had made it as far as the airport. In fact, I was in my seat and the flight was about to take off. And in that moment I made a decision: that I couldn't be away for five days getting beaten. I knew I was *already* beaten. I called the steward and said: 'I've got to get off.' Then I got off. And I went home. To go through with that action of getting off the plane showed how little I could do my job any more. 'That is it', I felt. 'It's gone.' Perhaps I was the instigator of my own eventual demise, but I just knew I couldn't win any more.

For a year or so I went through the motions. You know that feeling when your hands go really cold and you can't move them, all through nerves? I was feeling that more and more. I was unhappy with what I was attempting to achieve, and even unhappier with the fact that I wasn't ever going to achieve it. There were no positives. I was becoming less and less prepared for games, and I'd turn up later and later. I'd leave events earlier and earlier, too. I went to a couple like the Pro Tour events that were always on Saturdays and Sundays, and while previously I'd book three nights in a hotel, it got to the point where I didn't even bother booking a hotel room for the Sunday night because I knew I'd lose on the Saturday and be home by the Sunday.

I remember playing in a World Championship qualifier I'd put no preparation into at all; I simply turned up because it was 'the thing to do', just in case I got lucky. I lost to some-one whose name I don't even remember. You need the guts to compete and I'd lost my guts. I just didn't want to do it any more. If you're lucky in your work, you know what it's like to really relish it and feel excited by it. I'd felt that, once – I'd get up on the morning of a major final and I'd think to myself: 'I cannot wait until seven o'clock! Come on!' But I'd lost that. And I knew it wasn't coming back.

Eventually I had to face what was happening. I was leaving the K2 Leisure Centre in Crawley one afternoon, Donna in the driving seat with me in the passenger seat. There was total silence in the car. The event had not gone well. The only thing that had prevented my defeat that day being humiliating was the fact that humiliation generally hinges on some sort of loss of self-esteem, and my self-esteem had been at rock bottom before I'd even got on the oche.

As we pulled out of the carpark, Donna stopped the car, looked at me and said: 'You do know you'll never throw another dart professionally, don't you?'

'You might be right,' I said.

And she was right. So that's where it ended. All the wins, all the glories, all the highs of my career as a professional darts player. The whole thing crumbled to dust in a West Sussex carpark. I'd heard people describe Crawley as the place where dreams go to die, but I'd never thought they meant it literally.

In summary: I retired.

Retirement isn't something any pro takes lightly, but whereas I retired when I was thirty-eight many players keep on into their sixties and beyond. Darts is a sport that's all about replication – making the same throw time and time again – and as long as you've got a functioning arm you can make an impression, but it's also true that there's a golden period in anyone's life when they can do it best. Don't be distracted by the likes of Phil Taylor, who's a total outlier in terms of everything human beings do, and was good for so very, very long. For mortals like you and me there's a timeframe in which you have your peak.

If you're a footballer your best years are almost always likely to be between your teens and late twenties, but in darts performance is less dependent on your whole body's fitness, which for some participants is a blessing in disguise. Dennis Priestley once said that he believed any world-class darts player has ten years at the top, and I reckon he's right. Where those ten years come, however, is a different matter. Michael van Gerwen, for instance, started early but has possibly peaked in his early thirties. And if you look at other youngsters of today who've been playing a while – James Wade and Adrian Lewis spring to mind – you'd probably have to accept that they were better in their twenties than they are in their thirties. Dennis Priestley himself, on the other hand, didn't enter professional darts until he was forty but he hit the ground running. John Lowe famously said, following Priestley's first major triumph in 1991: 'I met this man a few months ago and he was just a county player, now he's the world champion.' Not only that, but despite his own theory Priestley had himself a pretty impressive twenty-year run – he was a force to be reckoned with into his sixties.

So that all ties in with *my* theory that darts is one of the rare sports where the later you start, the more chance you have of being able to continue your success. John Lowe and Bobby George didn't pick up a dart until they were grown men. If Priestley had started when he was twenty, I don't think he'd have had that lengthy run. One of the reasons for this is that there's a lot to be said for experiencing success at a slightly more advanced age – if you're twenty-five and you suddenly win a hundred grand you might throw half at a car and the other half at booze, nightclubs and whatever else. Everything past forty is a little bit more sedate, and a big first win is more likely to go on a kitchen extension.

Nonetheless, regardless of whether your decline is steep or takes place over the course of several years, when your time comes, you know it. It's interesting to see how different players cope when their own time comes.

Someone who's handled it really well is my friend and darts commentator Mark Webster – he's not officially retired but he no longer has a tour card and he doesn't really have the stomach he once did. He's working hard on his game to get back, but he kind of knows it may never happen – I hope he has one last crack. He's not what you'd call an all-time great (he's a former world champion from 2008, but not someone who automatically springs to mind as one of the best players the world's ever seen). And you know those people who make you say, 'He'll be a natural for TV'? To be frank he's not one of those at all.

But while he's never been the most charismatic player or the greatest success of all time, he's articulate and he's got a fantastic knowledge and understanding of the game, and he's worked really hard on getting himself opportunities within Sky Sports, ITV and the BBC. That way he knows he doesn't have to work a nine to five, but at the same time he's also a qualified plumber, and he still does enough of that to make sure things are ticking over. On any given week when there's

Sky Sports darts, people will see him in front of camera or in the commentary box, but what they don't know is that come Monday afternoon he might be up to his elbows in God-knows-what. I've never told Mark this, but I rather admire him – he has a drive to succeed unlike anything I think I ever had. He's a good human being.

The story of Ronnie Baxter, however, is a little sad. He's one of the most relentless winners in the game: he won in excess of fifty events worldwide in a career spanning from the mid-eighties to the mid-2000s, and was runner-up in the World Masters, World Matchplay, and the World Championship. But when his time came, he just couldn't let go. He'd become 'the draw', just like I had in my later days as a pro.

And he hadn't spent his money wisely, so he had little to show for how well he'd done. In the world of darts he was a threat for decades, but the last I heard he was delivering parcels for Amazon. I'm not saying he's been let down, but the demise of Ronnie Baxter is a lesson for everyone. Once you start falling, stopping that slide can seem impossible. He should be on the exhibition circuit and at the forefront of people's minds, rather than only coming up when people say: 'Do you remember Ronnie Baxter?'

Sadly, there are many decent blokes and great players who find themselves in Ronnie's position. I've known so many players over the years who've been and gone – they can't win any more, so they can't afford to pay for the right to play, or fund the flights and hotels necessary in order to compete in Germany or wherever. When the placings dry up, so does the sponsorship: you're no longer a commodity, you no longer sell twenty thousand sets of darts a year or ten thousand shirts a year. You'll sell seventy sets of darts and nine shirts.

Before I eventually retired there was a moment when I, too, was looking at this sort of future. I knew that I was running a business, and that I needed to earn money through that business in order to live. But the more I kept turning up at events, the more money I kept losing – I wasn't winning, but the cost of the hotels, flights, petrol and everything else stayed the same.

So many players in that situation feel like they have just one option: carry on and hope that things turn. Do you know what? Things don't turn. There might be a last hurrah where you've done nothing for six months and you get through a few rounds of an event through a series of flukes in the draw, or a series of lucky wins, and all of a sudden you find yourself in the quarter-finals, but then you get outplayed. Even though you're there, you and everyone else knows you can't win it. Everyone knows next week you're more likely to get beaten in the second round, yet again, than make the finals. And that's exactly what happens. People know you're finished. And you believe it too. But what else can you do? Players just carry on, and it's horrible to see.

Without things like commentary, darts exhibitions, corporate events and my darts school I'm certain I'd have found myself in the same position as 99 per cent of players who hit the same wall I did. My options meant that retirement from professional darts was a possibility, and rather less of a leap into the unknown than it might otherwise have been.

Even during my professional career Sky had asked me if I'd be interested in doing commentary. I'd told them I didn't want to do that until I retired, but I did a couple of test runs (including the

2011 World Championship) and knew there could be a future there. I would no longer be competing as a pro, but I knew there was a way to stay in that world. Luckily, as well as knowing Sky would probably take me on, I also knew I was sought after in the exhibition and corporate world and that I could get some work there, even after hanging up my darts competitively.

I threw my last competitive dart at the age of thirty-eight, and these days I'm happy I can still work in and around the darts world, meaning that I can build up enough of a nest egg to ensure I avoid becoming one of these seventy-year-olds touting himself out on Twitter or whatever social media site it'll be when I'm that old. I don't want to be that player; I don't want to be that human being. These days I still work for my money and I still love what I do, but most importantly I'm still involved in a sport I've been obsessed by from the age of ten.

I think I've made the absolute best of my retirement. I'm now more in demand than I've ever been, which is incredible. I've made a name for myself away from the oche so effectively that I know some people who are new to darts have no idea I was once a professional player myself. People simply see me as a commentator, and I think that's testament to how well I've stepped into my new role. So I don't regret retiring when I did. Maybe if I'd made different decisions there could have been a world title for me somewhere, but we'll never know what might have been.

Unless … Maybe I could give it another go?

Actually, I should be clear here: I will not, under any circumstances be giving it 'another go'. There was a rumour a year or so back that I'd be getting back into professional darts, and while I've still got no idea how it started, the speed with which it rocketed through social media was rather terrifying. Within an hour I had a guy from the *Daily Star* inboxing me to ask for the first interview of my comeback. And there was, actually, a split second when I thought: 'Hold on. This might have a bit of mileage.' It was just a little flicker in my mind. It came and went in a moment. I won't lie, there was also a flicker of: 'What kind of money could I make from this?'

The fact that my first thought was about money suggests to me that the whole thing would have been doomed: I would have been going back in for entirely the wrong reasons. Equally, there was the question of whether, in The Cursed Year, I could really have competed. The answer was a big no. I play against Michael van Gerwen, Barney, Taylor and the rest in exhibitions and events year in, year out. Can I beat them? Yes, if I'm fortunate to get them on an off day. But I couldn't beat them in a meaningful game – I just can't hold it together any more. My guts would go. My composure would go. Those numb, nervous fingers I had to retire to get away from would be back in an instant. I just couldn't do it. And in my heart of hearts, I wouldn't want to.

21.

THE
COMMENTARY
BOX

Darts started picking up a big TV following in the 1970s, but in 2021 it's bigger than ever, with Sky having confirmed that it's their second-most-watched sport (after a little-known endeavour you might have heard of called football). At the heart of any good televised darts tournament is decent commentary, and as a darts pro turned pundit for stations like Sky I've felt the effect of decent (and not-so-decent) commentary both in front of the camera and behind it.

Nobody will tell you this when you're starting out, but you don't even need to be on TV to get an idea of what it's like to be on the receiving end of commentary. If you've ever played darts in a pub or a club you'll have heard the muttering and murmuring and experienced the strange sensation of onlookers passing comment on your ability. From the moment you're playing in events you're always hearing critiques. Full-on TV commentary is similar, except this time the pub's got hundreds of thousands of people in it.

At the point when I was getting into commentary someone told me that one thing many good radio DJs have in common is that even when they're not on air they'll have a persistent internal monologue rattling around in their heads, meaning that they comment on their daily lives as if broadcasting to an audience.

The ability to keep thinking and keep talking, even when there's nothing of note actually happening, helps them stay sharp and avoid 'dead air' when they're in the studio. That struck me as a great idea, but it wasn't until last year when I started learning to drive that I discovered I did exactly the same thing, and if it hadn't been for my fantastic and rather straight-talking instructor Ruth I might never have known. 'Fuck me, Wayne,' she said, 'how about we leave the commentary for Sky Sports and concentrate on the bloody road?'

Well, that told me. I do still find the commentator in my head going ten-to-the-dozen when I'm watching a game on the TV, but I try to keep it to a minimum. In truth the best tips on commentating will always come from the greats, and I can't mention commentary greats without making reference to the masterly Sid Waddell. The son of a miner, he went to Cambridge University, and was surely destined for greatness in a very different career, but through a series of strange events he found himself becoming The Voice of Darts for many decades. By his own admission he was also an absolutely useless darts player, but he was gracious enough to leave that side of things to the pros.

One of my true best friends is the fantastic human being and even better commentator Rod Studd: a scholar, a border-line genius and my sometime sidekick, who had a stroke last year and was laid up for some time while he recovered – I really missed working with him during that terrible year. Rod once told me that back in the day he was backstage at a big television event and found good old Sid sat in a corner muttering to himself before a game.

'You alright, mate?' Rod asked.

'Oh yes,' Sid replied. 'I'm just practising my ad-libs.'

And I'm sorry to go the full Wizard of Oz on you here but, yes, many of the witty one-liners, jocular utterances and classic zingers you'll hear from great commentators (and myself) have, in fact, been prepared in advance. Sorry, but there it is.

We all do it. Why leave these things to chance? You know you'll be working on a certain game or with a certain player, and you prepare an absolute pearler. When the game starts you sit tight. You bide your time until, at the perfect moment, you just let it go – softly, without making a big thing of it. And then you watch it land. Delivering the perfect hilarious quip as a commentator is a lot like throwing a dart. (Not that you'd have guessed if you ever saw Waddell play.)

And hold onto your ruby slippers because I'm about to take you even further behind the curtain: the Notes app on my phone is full of generic commentary one-liners. I'm looking through it as I write these words and there are some classics in there.

Here's one: 'They're going to need an umbrella here – it's raining 180s.' I'm giving that a 7/10 – on an objective level it's crap, but I do feel it deserves a chortle, if little more.

Another: 'He's on fire, he wants to watch he doesn't melt the tungsten in his hand.' Yes, I know, it's 3/10 at best, but hear me out: 'And just for those who don't know, the melting point for tungsten is 3,422 degrees centigrade.' I don't like to blow my own trumpet, and to be frank I gave up trying in my late teens, but the extra detail in that second part surely lifts the whole thing to at least an 8/10.

I'll use both of those one day, plus some others that will undoubtedly spring to mind in the moment – the 'BULLSEYE' catchphrase that seems to follow me round wasn't an intentional utterance, just something that evolved. But I've got plenty of prepared gems in my Notes app. I'm not so sure about some of the entries lower down on the list. I've no idea what was on my mind when I wrote down, 'He's treading the stage like a lame kitten, I think he needs a cuddle', but you never know when a player might, indeed, begin to resemble a wobbly miniature cat.

The most important aspect of commentating is that you need to tell an audience not only what's happening, but why. As a commentator you're not providing an audio description for the visually impaired – you're there to provide insight and context. My mantra is 'informative and fun'. And it's the informative part that really makes a difference.

When I'm watching darts as a viewer I want to know *why* someone is missing that treble 20 when normally they're a safe pair of hands. And there always is a reason. Not so long ago Devon Petersen, one of the most improved players at that point, was playing Michael van Gerwen. He was brilliant on every segment, but at double 16, when it counted, darts were dipping. The context for that is that he just wasn't throwing the dart firmly enough, and the context for *that* is that Devon was hesitant. For a different player, missing double 16 could have a different cause. Stephen Bunting stands so far over to the right that he's cutting across to hit the double 16, which means that if he misses with his first dart on the outside, he's obscuring some of the target for the next dart, so he has to move and regain his composure.

Meanwhile, there's the time Phil Taylor famously lost in the 2016 world final to Gary Anderson. By this point Phil was generally not as dominant or as good as he used to be, and in this game he was making more mistakes than we'd ever seen from him, one of which was during the final when he was trying to hit a double 16. The darts just kept spiralling to the left. Here's the context for Phil: the way he throws, the darts roll up the thumb on release and spin in the air, like a bullet – and that spinning is what keeps a bullet straight. But if he threw with less purpose, as he was that day, the darts wouldn't fly straight, and that's why he was missing those 32s to the left.

Look, is all this technique stuff interesting? I put it to you that yes, it is interesting. I know you probably feel like the book peaked with the vinaigrette joke in the Travel chapter, but all I ask is that you keep the faith and plough on. You've made it this far.

I suppose the main point about commentary providing context is that knowing what's come *before* helps you truly understand what's happening *now*. Each game of darts is like one episode of a long-running soap opera: entertaining in its own right, but better when you know who's had it off with whom, the twists and turns of the knicker-factory ownership, and precisely why the sale of the fruit and veg stall has a special significance.

In fact the more I think about it, the easier it is to match darts professionals with notorious soap characters. Peter Manley, for instance, would do anything to win a game: JR Ewing. Ian White always looks like he's going to win, but always ends up failing, faltering at the last moment: Gail Platt. Ronny and his brother Kim Huybrechts: the Mitchell brothers, without the crack habit. (In fairness they're nothing like the Mitchells but they are brothers, and that's enough for me.)

Speaking of appearances, when I'm commentating my day always starts with a decision on what to wear. There are various rules in place when it comes to appearing on Sky Sports – nothing stripy, nothing too bright, but also nothing too dark, nothing too attention grabbing. As you may have guessed, I've been told in no uncertain terms that Sky Sports is absolutely not the place for the multi-coloured polyester spectacles with which I'm most closely associated, so it's dress shirts all the way when I'm due in front of the camera.

'Some commentators dress for show,' I was told, 'but *we* dress for business.'

'What if my business is spreading joy?' I asked.

Blank faces. I got the message: Sky Sports pundits and presenters are there to be listened to, not to be looked at.

I'm of that certain age where the primary appeal of any shirt has ceased to have anything to do with fashion and is now firmly based on comfort. For this reason I turn to Marks & Spencer. These days M&S is a chain best known for its dizzying proliferation of pig-themed confectionery, but its clothing range still hits the spot, and more importantly it adheres to Sky's rather miserly clothing budget, so I buy my shirts in bulk, a dozen at a time. (Note to self: investigate upping that clothing budget.)

The only trouble with bulk buying is that on any given day I have no idea which shirts are actually going to fit. I look at a bourbon biscuit and I put on half a pound; I look away from the biscuit tin and *lose* a pound. For this reason I have a wardrobe full of shirts going from a 15-inch neck to a 17½, and trousers with waists ranging from 34 inches to 42. The upshot: my wardrobe is stacked with nearly a hundred shirts in myriad sizes and any colour as long as it's boring: black, maroon, mid blue, light blue, sky blue (yes, there is a difference between this and light blue), navy blue or royal blue.

The most important thing to know about actually sitting in the commentary box is that if there are any cats you wish to swing, you'll need to go outside. Depending on the venue you're likely looking at a room seven feet wide by six feet deep, and once you've accounted for all the monitors, wires and production nonsense you're left with the distinct feeling of having been shut in a cupboard. Not a particularly exciting cupboard either, until the players start throwing. The main thrill you'll get in the commentary box is from the knowledge that at some point – never at a predictable time, to keep us on our toes and engender a sense of mystery and wonder – someone will appear with a platter of sandwiches.

Now I've done alright in life, I've been wined and dined in the poshest restaurants, and I've worked my way towards a lifestyle that allows me to afford the occasional expensive night out, but one thing rings true whether you're a prince or a pauper: you simply cannot go wrong with free sandwiches. And when I see that tempting buffet of bready goodness I just can't control myself. Very often Sky will come back from a commercial break and I'll be midway through absolutely devolishing – that's devouring, and demolishing – a tuna or coronation chicken sandwich, trying not to give the game away that I've got a mouth full of granary. Luckily I'm a quick eater so I've never yet spoken with a totally full face.

CORONATION CHICKEN THOUGHTS: The thing with this filling is that it was commissioned to mark the Queen's coronation in 1953 and I'm sure at the time they thought it would be a flash in the pan, but sixty-eight years later it's still there. The Bob Anderson of the sandwich world. Stands the test of time and in its day a champion; the sandwich to which all other sandwiches aspire.

TUNA OPINION: Some people claim fish has no business being between two slices of bread, to which I offer just three words – fish, finger, sandwich.

(I do love a fish-finger sandwich.)

In much the same way as parents are supposed to pretend they don't have a favourite child, it's expected that a commentator will love each of their commentees equally, but in practice it's just a fact that some of those players are fun to chat about while others are a little more on the challenging side.

The best players to commentate on are the exciting ones: Michael van Gerwen, Gary Anderson, Nathan Aspinall, Gerwyn Price. To be frank, if your surname starts with an A or involves some variation on Gerwyn or Gerwen you should quit your job now and get into darts because I can't wait to critique your playing for an audience of millions. The pleasing thing about each of those players is that they truly respond to what's happening in the game – as a commentator you can screech and holler all you like, but nothing compares to the sight of a grown human being cavorting around the stage like a headless chicken.

When someone plays darts with flair and joy, I get more of a kick out of it as a commentator, and I'm sure you get more enjoyment as a viewer. Think about football – a goal is always more exciting when the striker's pulling his top over his head, somersaulting or doing a reverse Macarena on one leg while Clive Tyldesley is sounding on the verge of an aneurysm.

Audiences don't want to see cool, calm and collected when someone's won the World Championship, and neither do commentators. We want to see a performance. We want emotion. Most of all, we want to see a man or woman getting so excited they look like they're about to soil themselves on live TV, and I'm not shitting *you* when I say impromptu defecation on the oche must surely be the Holy Grail of any sports commentator. (Yes, I'd tell the audience politely and eloquently what had happened ... before erupting into a ball of shitty spouting nonsense.)

What I absolutely do not want to see is someone underplaying their success. Nonchalance is something I'm prepared to tolerate from two groups of people: 1950s Hollywood superstars and the French. As far as darts players go, they've tried for years to get where they are, and every win opens a door to somewhere new and exciting. So it's fine to respond with a little more than a shrug and a tentative thumbs up.

We're definitely going through a period in darts where humility and 'apologeticness' seem to be the order of the day – often you'll see someone winning a leg and as soon as their darts are in the board they turn to the crowd and hold their hands up as if to say they're sorry! What's that all about? I want to see your hands when you're caught up in a bank heist, not when you're about to win a quarter of a million quid. I want to commentate on people who give something back to their audience. I get that we're all different. Also, I just don't like it.

The biggest gripe for me, though, doesn't concern players not giving back to the audience; it's commentators who give too *much* back to the players.

There's a phenomenon I like to call Mates Commentary, and if you've been watching televised sport for a couple of decades you'll probably know what I'm getting at. In any number of sports there's been a rise in the ex-professional-turned-commentator. (Yes, I know I'm on thin ice here but bear with me.) We're now in an era where former players of a sport go into the commentary box or find a spot on the punditry sofa, and I accept that there are clear benefits to this. The sense of context and insight I mentioned earlier, for example, is something only a former professional can really deliver. But that comes at a price.

Particularly in darts, where the exhibition circuit means pros and ex-pros are frequently still hanging out together, you'll hear commentary by people – I'm offering no names here because I quite like my teeth as they are – who twenty-four hours later will be sharing a pint with the players they're supposed to be objectively discussing. The result? Biased commentary for the benefit of their mate. It's subtle, but if you know what to look for you'll spot it.

One frequent observation is 'I think they can win this' when the player in question is throwing with all the grace of a cat stuck in a harpsichord and wouldn't even claim themselves that they stood a hope of winning the game. If the commentator's got two mates competing against each other, you'll hear platitudes like 'Oh, it'll be a great game – either could win'. It's doing a disservice to the viewer. You can't lie to the viewer just because someone's your mate. If it's two mates, don't say, 'Oh, it'll be a great game, either could win'. Come on, you've got an opinion, let it out.

Also, it's actually doing a disservice to the player you're trying to help out. Most of all, you're lying on live national television. All because you don't want to offend your mate. Maybe it's just me, but when I'm on commentary duties I feel I'm there to do a job, and that means being honest with the viewer. Particularly as when the viewer's seeing someone throw their way through the worst game of their life, they know exactly what they're seeing.

I still cling to the idea of 'harsh but fair when it's called for'. I remember commentating on a match involving Kevin Painter who, bless him, was having a stinker of a game. I just had to bite the bullet. 'I'm a great friend of Kev,' I said, 'but this just isn't good enough to win a game and he's going to have to start playing better. I hate to say it, but Kevin's best days are behind him.' Did I like seeing how he was playing, and did I enjoy making sure Sky's viewers were left in no doubt as to Kev's predicament? No, on both counts.

But here's the thing: if you're good enough mates with someone to feel like you want to protect them, surely that also means you're good enough mates for them to accept the occasional bit of tough truth-saying. Afterwards our relationship just carried on: he didn't bin me off, because he knew my assessment of the situation had been fair, and he knew I'd been telling the truth. I mean, he didn't exactly thank me either, but I was hardly expecting the arrival of a flower bouquet and a stuffed teddy.

To be absolutely honest, reflecting on that I can only conclude that Kev's a bigger man than me. During my run as a pro I did once or twice take exception to snippy commentary. Oscar Wilde once said: 'There is only one thing in the world worse than being talked about, and that is not being talked about.' I don't know much about old Oscar's prowess on the oche, but I do know he never had to put up with Sid Waddell (a) getting his name wrong and (b) inventing a negative darting term in his honour. But that's what happened to me.

Sid would *always* pronounce my name 'Mardel', like I was some sort of French coastal holiday destination, and most woundingly of all he noted on live TV that there were times when I was under pressure that my attempts at a treble 20 would drift left, in the direction of a treble 5. In Sid's eyes, to hit a 15 once in a game may be misfortune but to hit it repeatedly looked like carelessness or, as he chose to term it, evidence of 'The Mardel Drift'.

The first time I heard what he'd been saying about me, I wasn't happy. When I found out he'd done it again, I sought out a video recording and there it all was: I could hit a 180 and he'd say nothing, then I'd get a treble 5 – like plenty of players do – and he was banging on about the Mardel Drift: 'Here Mardel goes again!' I felt like this was unfair, and I knew it was time to get Waddell on the phone.

'Sid, mate,' I began. 'Look, we love each other but this has got to stop. I've played well, I've won a game, I've hit good scores and I'm finding this off-putting. You're making me think about my game, but that's not what you're there for.'

He said he'd watch the game back, then get back to me. Later that day the phone rang. 'Well, Wayne, I've looked back and you did hit a five.' He wasn't going to budge. The next game came along and, wouldn't you know it, along came a reference to the Mardel Drift. Just once, though, this time. Maybe something about my phone call had made him think twice.

I mean no disrespect to Sid. Growing up I considered his voice synonymous with darts, in the same way that Murray Walker was the voice of motor racing and the recently deceased and already much missed Peter Allis was the voice of golf. Back then, of course, there were only three channels and a limited number of voices on offer, and now there are a million different commentators offering their thoughts on two million different sports across three million different channels, but I'm not one to question progress, particularly as it's the rise of multichannel stations like Sky that's putting food on my table.

I don't know whether I'll ever quite get to the iconic status of a Sid Waddell or a Murray Walker. The TV critic Clive James once wrote that 'even in moments of tranquillity, Murray Walker sounds like a man whose trousers are on fire' and that feels like something to aim for.

I may rarely reach that level of intensity, but I'll always do my best to capture the true excitement of being in the middle of the action. There have been times after a live broadcast when I've read Twitter and there are people going: 'Jesus, Mardle was excited tonight.'

To me, that's the highest compliment. Of course I'm excited – darts is my life, I've been living and breathing the sport since I was ten, and even if my trousers aren't on fire it's my mission now just as much as it's ever been to share that excitement as much as I can, and inspire the same excitement in others.

I can't imagine what my life would have been like without darts in it. I've experienced dizzying highs and crushing lows, played against the best in the world and beaten most of them, and lived a life my ten-year-old self couldn't ever have imagined. Even in my late forties I struggle to get my head around it all.

Would I change anything? Well, there's a good line on regret coined by former professional Scott Rand, who, back in 2011 when he was still starting out, managed to win a couple of matches on TV, putting him in the semi-finals. 'I'm going to turn professional,' he announced and, true to his word, he packed in his job the very next day. Six months later he was out of the game – those matches on TV had been *it*, and the truth was he just wasn't good enough, often enough or for long enough. His became something of a cautionary tale in darting circles, but reflecting on it all later on he famously said: 'I don't want any regrets. Regret is a wasted emotion.'

We darts players aren't exactly well known for our profundity, but he touched on something so real in that statement. Even though his prowess on the oche didn't leave much impression on the darting world, those words have become rather hallowed among professionals. Perhaps that's not the legacy he might have hoped for, but it's something quite special none-theless. Even today you hear it a lot behind the scenes, and it means so much to us because it came from the lips of a darts player.

Maybe if I were to do my time again I'd make a few tweaks to the story here and there: I'd have joined the PDC a year or two earlier, I might have cut down on the Bargain Buckets during the 2000s, and I'd think twice about throwing a dart through a fan's hand, for instance. But do I regret a minute? I look at the friends I've made and the life I've created for myself in this extraordinary sport and my answer's simple: not a chance.